WITHDRAWN

HARVARD HISTORICAL MONOGRAPHS

HARVARD HISTORICAL MONOGRAPHS
XXI

PUBLISHED UNDER THE DIRECTION OF THE DEPARTMENT
OF HISTORY FROM THE INCOME OF

THE ROBERT LOUIS STROOCK FUND

324.4
R119e

The Election to the Russian Constituent Assembly of 1917

OLIVER HENRY RADKEY

Fellow in Slavic Studies
Hoover Institute
1947-1948

Cambridge: 1950

HARVARD UNIVERSITY PRESS

COPYRIGHT 1950

BY THE PRESIDENT AND FELLOWS OF HARVARD COLLEGE

PRINTED IN THE UNITED STATES OF AMERICA

LONDON : GEOFFREY CUMBERLEGE

OXFORD UNIVERSITY PRESS

TO JAKOBA AND INGRID

CAT Dec20'50

100940

ACKNOWLEDGMENT

THE GENEROSITY of the Hoover Institute and the resources of the Hoover Library have made it possible to prepare this study. Professor Michael Karpovich and the Department of History of Harvard University have undertaken its publication. The author is grateful to his friends for all they have done in bringing to fruition a project begun years ago in the libraries of Europe and completed in residence at the Hoover Library. No higher tribute can be paid this institution than to say that as a place for research it is as admirable as the character of the man who founded it.

The manuscript has been read by Professor Karpovich and by Professor Anatole Mazour of Stanford University. The amendments made as a result of their suggestions and corrections have enabled the author to fit his specialized study more securely into the framework of Russian actuality. Even more than their advice, however, their words of encouragement have been appreciated.

The manuscript was also examined and approved for publication by Professors Brinton and Fainsod. For their kindness and consideration the author is duly grateful.

To Professor H. Malcolm Macdonald of the University of Texas, personal friend and specialist in a related field, the author is indebted for invaluable counsel and assistance in getting this study under way.

OLIVER HENRY RADKEY

Palo Alto, California
August 1948

CONTENTS

THE ELECTION TO THE RUSSIAN
CONSTITUENT ASSEMBLY OF 1917

CHAPTER I

THE SETTING

No DEFINITIVE STUDY of the election to the All-Russian Constituent Assembly in the fall and winter of 1917 has yet been made. Today, on the thirtieth anniversary of that mournful occasion when more than forty million votes were cast in vain, it seems less than ever likely that such a study will or can be made, for the obstacles that lie in the way are so numerous and forbidding that even Soviet investigators, with all the advantages that location and official favor can give, have despaired of the task and have consigned it to oblivion.[1]

Yet an attempt at reconstruction of what took place will always have historical validity, if only because this is the one real election in the experience of the Russian people — real, that is, in the sense that it was a fundamentally free election, contested by definitely organized and sharply divergent parties, on the basis of universal, equal, direct, and secret suffrage. It is true that it was held during one of the great crises of Russian history, and hence reflected a mood less stable than that which would have prevailed in normal times; yet merely to record the will of a great people at a crucial stage of its development is to preserve something of

[1] Tsentrarkhiv, Arkhiv Oktiabrskoi Revoliutsii (hereinafter cited as AOR), *1917 g. v dokumentakh i materialakh*, ed. M. N. Pokrovski and Ia. A. Iakovlev: *Vserossiiskoe Uchreditelnoe Sobranie*, ed. I. S. Malchevski, (Moscow-Leningrad, 1930), p. xxviii. As further evidence of the difficulties encountered, the author of the present study may cite his own experience. In assembling the materials used here he found it necessary to draw on the resources of no less than six widely spaced libraries: the Russian Archives Abroad in Prague, the Marx-Engels-Lenin Institute at Moscow, the Moscow Public Library, the Bibliothèque de la Guerre at Vincennes, the Widener Library of Harvard University, and the Hoover Library in California. Of these only the Widener Library could have been dispensed with; each of the others contained indispensable information not available in the other four. Finally, there is certain valuable information that is not to be found in any of these libraries.

enduring value, quite apart from the disclosure of certain tendencies in the vast Eurasian empire which are in no sense transitory but are of permanent significance. How, then, can the obscurity that has surrounded this historic event be explained?

The abortive nature of the ill-fated assembly is one reason for the neglect of the election which produced it. Lenin dissolved the Constituent Assembly by force after a single session on January 5, 1918,[2] amid the plaudits, open or secret, of both the extremes of Russian political life. Of more fateful significance was the fact that while the democratic parties heaped opprobrium upon him for this act of despotism, their following showed little inclination [3] to defend an institution which the Russian people had ceased to regard as necessary to the fulfillment of its cherished desires. For the Constituent Assembly, even before it had come into existence, had been caught in a back-eddy of the swiftly flowing stream of revolutionary developments and no longer commanded the interest and allegiance of the general population which alone could have secured it against a violent death.

Even had its existence not been so swiftly terminated, however, the greater interest in the assembly would not necessarily have guaranteed a clearer record of its origins. The election, or rather the elections, had taken place under the most unfavorable circumstances. Quite apart from the vastness of Russia and the general unfamiliarity with democratic procedure, the mere fact that the election was held less than nine months after one revolution and less than three weeks after another rendered the task of administration exceedingly difficult. Set for November 12–14 (25–27), the vote came off as scheduled in most of the country, but in a number of districts preparations had not been completed and postponement was necessary, with the result that the balloting was

---

[2] January 18 by the Western calendar. For the sake of convenience, and also because it continued to be official until 1918, the Old Style has been retained throughout this study.

[3] At least at this time. Later on, in the first stages of the civil war, the SR's whipped up considerable popular sentiment against the Bolsheviks on the grounds that the Soviet government had violated the will of the people in dissolving the Constituent Assembly.

strung out over a period of three months and, in some cases, never took place at all.[4] The returns came in unevenly, for the electoral machinery remained in the hands of commissions appointed by the Provisional Government after that regime itself had been supplanted by the Bolsheviks; as a consequence, unity of administration was lost in the clash of authority. The system of communications had become disrupted, especially the telegraph, making it difficult for the *uezd* [5] electoral commissions to report to the district commissions,[6] not to speak of the difficulties encountered by the latter in communicating with the All-Russian Commission on Affairs Pertaining to the Election of the Constituent Assembly in Petrograd. And even if the results were known locally, that does not mean that record of them exists today, for precisely at the time they were being announced, the Bolshevik campaign against the press reached its height and newspapers were being suppressed right and left (in a double sense).[7] Add to these factors the dreadful incubus of a long and exhausting war

[4] N. V. Sviatitski, *Kogo russkii narod izbral svoimi predstaviteliami?* (Moscow, n.d.), pp. 3-4. See also below, p. 6.

[5] The term *uezd* has been retained here as its nearest equivalent, the word "county," somehow does not fit. On the other hand, *guberniia* will be rendered by "province" and *volost* by "canton." In the Russian administrative system, the largest unit was the province, consisting of a number of *uezds*, each of which in turn was subdivided into cantons, and each of these into villages. The electoral set-up followed roughly the same lines, the largest unit being known as *okrug* (district) rather than *guberniia* (province). In most instances, however, "district" and "province" were one and the same.

[6] "Chleny Uchreditelnago Sobraniia ot Saratovskoi gubernii," *Vestnik Privolzhskago Kraia*, no. 2 (December 16, 1917). This editorial cites the example of Kamyshin *uezd*. Another type of trouble in the same province is indicated in the following telegram, sent by the chairman of the Kuznetsk *uezd* commission on November 22 to the district commission in Saratov: "Ransacking of state liquor warehouse began in town today. Great deal of drunkenness. Population in panic. Plundering of banks and merchants impending. Work of *uezd* commission halted" (quoted in *Saratovskii Vestnik*, no. 251, November 23, 1917).

[7] As an illustration, the two papers cited in the foregoing footnote are actually one. The *Saratovskii Vestnik* was suppressed and had to reappear under a new title. Then it, too, was suppressed. Later on the Bolsheviks did better — one act of suppression was enough to close down a paper under any guise.

which bore down upon the Russian state and people with crushing weight, and the further devastating experience of the civil war that lay ahead, with all the loss entailed in respect to local records, and one will begin to understand why the facts concerning a general election, held in a great country as recently as 1917, should today be so largely unknown.

Only three investigations of fundamental significance to the study of this election have been published. Though thirty years have gone by, the basic work is still that of the Socialist Revolutionary deputy and electoral statistician, N. V. Sviatitski, who tabulated the returns, insofar as they were available to him, and analyzed them in reasonably objective fashion.[8] Lenin followed with a commentary on the election based upon the study of Sviatitski, which he took over without change as far as statistics were concerned, neither adding to them nor questioning their validity. Naturally, Lenin's interpretation was his own and differs markedly from that of Sviatitski, but his point of view was by no means as biased as one might expect, for he conscientiously sought in the figures the lessons they contained for his party, whether flattering or otherwise, and his deductions constitute a thoroughgoing and penetrating analysis of the results.[9] Years later, under the auspices of the Archives of the October Revolution, a study appeared which contains the stenographic report of the proceedings of the Constituent Assembly and sheds some further light, in the annotations and introduction, upon the election itself. The contribution is a modest one, however, since the original

[8] "Itogi vyborov vo Vserossiiskoe Uchreditelnoe Sobranie (predislovie)," *God russkoi revoliutsii (1917–1918g.g.)*: *Sbornik statei* (Moscow, 1918), pp. 104–119. This article was expanded somewhat and appeared in book form under the same title, *Itogi vyborov vo Vserossiiskoe Uchreditelnoe Sobranie* (Moscow, 1918). Both are rare. Lenin used the article, not the book, as material for his study. Sviatitski also published a pamphlet (no. 86 in the SR series) in answer to Bolshevik charges as to the counterrevolutionary composition of the assembly; this pamphlet is cited above, note 4. He also wrote short analyses for the *Delo Naroda* during the voting period. Sviatitski's writings have a mild SR slant.

[9] "Vybory v Uchreditelnoe Sobranie i diktatura proletariata," *Sochineniia* (2nd ed.; Moscow-Leningrad, 1930–1932), XXIV (1919), 631–649.

project of compiling a full set of returns which would supersede those of Sviatitski could not be carried through, the tangible gain being restricted to returns from four electoral districts which are missing in the earlier tabulation (Don Region, Stavropol, Orenburg, and the Transcaucasus). The editors also announced that they had been able to go beyond Sviatitski in a number of instances where his information was incomplete or inaccurate, but they did not publish their work of revision, simply incorporating it into the totals for the country at large.[10]

This is an unfortunate circumstance, for the present writer has also been able to improve the statistics of Sviatitski at a number of points, yet has no way of knowing what degree of coincidence may exist between his figures and those of the Soviet investigation. Consequently, there is no possibility of drawing all the information together and presenting totals for the country which would be definitive, even so far as the present status of research is concerned. Entire electoral districts are still missing, but in three cases, at least, the writer has succeeded in unearthing returns for districts which appear neither in Sviatitski's list nor in the Soviet supplement.[11] One of these is the Podolia district[12] in the Ukraine.[13]

[10] AOR, *Vserossiiskoe Uchreditelnoe Sobranie*, p. xxviii. They were able to verify his figures for 21 of the 55 districts included in the tabulation.

[11] See below, p. 12.

[12] Here electoral district and province are one, as is usually the case, so that a large and populous area is involved.

[13] *Robitnicha Gazeta* (organ of the central committee of the Ukrainian Social Democratic Party), no. 222 (January 6, 1918). Podolia will serve as an illustration of how difficult it is to assemble data pertaining to the election. Sviatitski not only did not have the returns but did not even know whether the voting had taken place; the blame he places on the "war" between the Bolsheviks and the Rada (*Itogi vyborov*, p. 38). The Ukrainian newspaper in which I found the figures states that the election was held on December 3–5, 1917, and that a total of 741,064 votes were cast in 9 of the 12 *uezds*, the other 3 not reporting. Yet if the vote as given for each party list is added up, the total is 830,260, indicating perhaps that one or more of the missing *uezds* had come in. The newspaper makes no attempt to explain the discrepancy. Later numbers contain no further information; the account was published on the day of the dissolution of the Constituent Assembly, and the whole matter appears subsequently to have become a dead issue.

No returns have yet been found for the Kaluga and Bessarabia districts of European Russia, nor for the three Far Eastern districts of Kamchatka, Iakutsk, and the Chinese Eastern Railroad, although balloting took place in each and the names of the victorious candidates are known.[14] Except for the city of Ekaterinodar, no election was held in the Kuban–Black Sea district of the North Caucasus, nor in the Terek–Daghestan area, and the same is true of all ten of the districts in Central Asia; approximately one hundred seats were thus left vacant in the Constituent Assembly.[15]

Bearing in mind these gaps in our knowledge, and remembering also that only partial returns are available for a number of districts, we can nevertheless obtain a clear picture of the results of the election. As we turn to them, the first thing that engages our attention is the multiplicity of parties vying for the favor of the Russian people. With some of these the Western reader is familiar; with others, he presumably is not. Only the basic distinctions can be pointed out here.

The socialist sector was divided into two camps — the Marxist and the Narodnik or Populist — and each of these was divided within itself. How the original Marxist movement, the Russian Social Democratic Workingmen's party, had fallen apart into the Menshevik and Bolshevik wings, and how these had grown further and further apart until by 1917 membership within the same party had become purely fictitious, is all a familiar story. It was a difference in temperament as much as in theory that divided the Russian Social Democrats: the Mensheviks were patient and cautious folk, who would not force the pace of events but would let the laws of capitalistic development work themselves

---

Even had interest been sustained, the wild times that ensued in the Ukraine might well have precluded the gathering of complete returns.

[14] See list of members of the Constituent Assembly in AOR, *Vserossiiskoe Uchreditelnoe Sobranie*, pp. 116–138, and foreword, pp. 114–115. The compilation of this list of more than 700 deputies is the most valuable service rendered by the Soviet investigation.

[15] M. V. Vishniak, *Vserossiiskoe Uchreditelnoe Sobranie* (Paris, 1932), pp. 91–92.

out. Nothing could be worse, they felt, than for a socialist party to come into power before society was ready for socialism, for in that case the socialist regime would be discredited in the eyes of its own followers in addition to encountering the desperate resistance of a still powerful propertied class. Until such time as capitalism had run its course in Russia and practically had fallen into the grave of its own digging, the Mensheviks would exploit the forms of the liberal state to build up the organization of the working class and educate it for the performance of its historic mission. Thus was their theory made to conform to their temperament. The Bolsheviks, on the other hand, were insurrectionary in spirit, conspiring to seize the power of state as the conscious vanguard of the proletariat and from that vantage ground to complete the organization of the toiling masses and bring in the socialist order of society.[16] Both groups were staunchly Marxist in ideology; Menshevism must not be confused with revisionism. If anything, the Bolsheviks were less hidebound and more given to experimentation than their rivals. The official line of the Menshevik Party lay decidedly to the left of the Majority Socialists in Germany, being comparable to that of the Austrian and Saxon Social Democrats.

The rival Narodnik or Populist school of socialism was nativist in inspiration and agrarian in emphasis. It held that Russia could arrive at socialism in her own way, building upon those hoary institutions and folk habits like the village commune which had

[16] In this connection a passage from Lenin's treatise on the election (p. 639) merits translation *in extenso*: "The opportunist gentlemen, among them the followers of Kautsky, are 'instructing' the people, in mockery of Marx's teaching, that the proletariat must first achieve a majority by means of universal suffrage, then on the basis of such a majority vote take over the government, and only then proceed to organize socialism on the foundation of this 'progressive' (others say 'pure') democracy. But we speak from the vantage-ground of Marxist doctrine *and the experience of the Russian Revolution* [italics are mine]: the proletariat must first overthrow the bourgeoisie and conquer *for itself* the power of state, then use this power — i.e., the dictatorship of the proletariat — as an instrument of its own class for the purpose of winning the sympathies of a majority of the toilers" (also quoted in Vishniak, p. 93*n*).

retarded or inhibited the development of a property consciousness on the part of the Russian people. In view of this fortuitous circumstance — fortuitous, that is, from the Narodnik viewpoint — Russia's society need not be subjected to the disintegrating influences of capitalist development or to the Marxist projection of the class war into the village.[17] It had broadened the Marxist concept of the class struggle by ranging the "toiling" peasantry (those who worked the soil without recourse to hired labor) and the "toiling" intelligentsia alongside the proletariat in the army of the exploited; in fact, it was much more concerned with the peasantry than with the proletariat. Its cardinal tenet was that "all the land should belong to all the people" — that is, that the usufruct (but not the ownership) of the land should be vested equally in those who worked it with their own hands. In simplest terms, the Narodniks were people who wanted to make a revolution in an overwhelmingly agrarian country and had to devise an ideology that would justify an appeal to what was by far the strongest subversive force in Tsarist Russia — the elemental discontent of the rural masses. Nothing was more certain than that this appeal would be made, and since the Marxists did not choose to make it, the Narodniks did. At the time of the first revolution (1905–1907) the Narodnik movement had split into two parties, the minority Popular Socialists drawing away from the majority Socialist Revolutionaries because of their aversion to the strident republicanism and taste for terrorism of the dominant faction. After the February Revolution in 1917 the Popular Socialists continued to be a very small though highly conscious group, while the Party of the Socialist Revolutionaries (PSR) swelled to enormous proportions.

Some salient features of this party — the largest in the country — may be pointed out for the benefit of the Western reader. The core of the PSR was the rural intelligentsia: the village scribes, the children of the priests, the employees of the *zemstvos* and coöperatives, and, above all, the village schoolteachers. The party's

[17] This the Narodniks abhorred above all else, desiring to preserve the solidarity of the peasantry, apart from the *kulak* element.

center of gravity lay not in the heart of Great Russia, in the region around Moscow, but to the southeast, in the black-earth zone and along the middle and lower Volga. The city of Saratov, sometimes called the "Athens of the Volga," had been associated with the earliest beginnings of the party and long had served it as a kind of intellectual capital. The SR ideology, partly, no doubt, because of its very vagueness, enjoyed tremendous popularity, and not only among the Great Russians: the Ukrainian intellectuals, intoxicated with the heady wine of nationalism, organized their own SR party with huge success, and along the middle Volga and between it and the Urals the movement spread to the native non-Russian populations, Finnish or Tatar, Orthodox or Mohammedan, assuming as it did so a nationalist or religious coloration.

It is conventional to regard all of the parties mentioned above as being socialistic, though the Marxists, for example, would deny that designation to the Narodniks. Turning now to the political camp which defended the institution of private property, we find the Constitutional Democrats, commonly known as "Kadets," standing virtually alone.[18] The conservative groups to the right of the Kadets in the Third and Fourth Dumas had been the products of a distorted electoral system and could not exist on the basis of universal, direct, and equal suffrage; they had simply vanished from the scene, being swallowed up for the most part by the Kadets.[19] The only rightist group with a truly popular following — the Union of Russian People — had either fallen apart as a result of the moral rottenness and material bankruptcy of the old regime or had been driven under cover to escape the fierce draught of the revolution. The scattered embers of this movement — one of whose slogans had been, "Beat the Jews and Save Russia!" — still glowed here and there on the Russian landscape and were by no means extinguished; the throne and the church still had their devoted adherents, and the Jews, their bitter enemies. But as an

---

[18] The Kadets' official name was *Narodnaia Svoboda* (People's Freedom) or *Partiia Narodnoi Svobody*.

[19] The chief of these conservative groups was the Octobrist. Others were the Progressive, Nationalist, and so on.

organized, All-Russian movement, the Union of Russian People had ceased to exist, even though locally it might contest the polls under various guises.

The Constitutional Democrats were a proud and influential party, numbering among their members the cream of the intellectual and business spheres of Russian society. Many university professors were Kadets, among them the party leader, P. N. Miliukov. A spirit of nationalism not untinged with imperialism pervaded the ranks of this party, and its leadership had seen in the war not so much a calamity as an opportunity to destroy the Teutonic hegemony over the Western and Southern Slavs and to acquire for Russia the Straits and Galicia. The party's inspiration was western, as was its orientation: it admired the institutions of France and Great Britain and fervently sustained the alliance against Germany and Austria. The party had not embraced republicanism until after the Tsar had lost his throne and, despite the semblance of unanimity achieved on that occasion,[20] undoubtedly contained within its ranks more than a few who preferred a constitutional monarchy. The Constitutional Democrats had their own scheme of land reform, under which the holdings of the peasantry would be enlarged through grants in perpetuity, the landowners being compensated by the state for their losses.[21]

[20] The VII party congress (March 25, 1917). See A. A. Kornilov, *Partiia Narodnoi Svobody* (*Istoricheskii ocherk*) (Petrograd, 1917), pp. 29–31, and "Partiia Narodnoi Svobody," *Sputnik izbiratelia v Uchreditelnoe Sobranie* (Petrograd, 1917), pp. 69–70. The Kadet historian writes as though monarchist sentiment had completely evaporated. Yet compare the attitude of Miliukov in the first days of the February Revolution. Thereafter, for some members at least, a republican solution became more a matter of expediency than an article of faith.

[21] These grants might be made either to societies or to individuals, as the peasants wished. The Kadets did not favor an enforced dissolution of the village commune. Their land program did not go as far toward establishing a regime of private property as one would expect. It occupied an intermediate position between the Stolypin legislation and the Narodnik program, the influence of which is palpably evident. See E. A. Morokhovets, *Agrarnye programmy rossiiskikh politicheskikh partii v 1917 godu* (Leningrad, 1929), pp. 141–153; text of program in *Programma Partii Narodnoi Svobody* (*Konstitutsionno-Demokraticheskoi*) (Petrograd, 1917), sec. vi, pp. 9–14.

These were the parties that fought the election to the Constituent Assembly. In the pages following, it is proposed, first, to set forth the results of the election, then to proceed to an analysis of these results, and thereafter to examine the conditions under which the balloting took place, with a view toward determining whether the results are valid or whether so much terrorism, intimidation, and knavery were practiced at the polls as to make the outcome of the election a caricature of the will of the Russian people. Finally, an attempt will be made to estimate the degree of consciousness of the voting public as it went to the polls.

CHAPTER II

ANALYSIS OF RETURNS FOR THE COUNTRY AT LARGE

As ALREADY has been intimated, the electoral statistics are in a deplorable condition, being widely dispersed and shot through with inaccuracies and contradictions. In tabulating the votes it is necessary to give the totals for the country at large in three columns, none of which has any claim to completeness. The first contains the figures of Sviatitski, just as he gave them.[1] The second column represents the work of the Soviet Archives of the October Revolution, regarding which so little is said as to preclude verification or integration of the results.[2] The third column embodies the research of this author, who has taken the other two studies as a basis for his own, supplementing them wherever possible in one of two ways: either by incorporation of returns hitherto missing or by substitution of more complete or more accurate returns for those that were given.[3] In the case of four electoral districts — Olonets, Esthonia, Podolia, and the Baltic Fleet — it has been possible to produce returns where none were available to Sviatitski (three of these are likewise missing in the Soviet compilation, and the fourth — Esthonia — quite possibly is missing). In respect to a number of other electoral districts — Arkhangelsk, Tver, Samara, Saratov, Ienisei, Chernigov, Poltava,

[1] The column was made up on the basis of returns from 54 out of 79 districts. "Itogi vyborov," *God russkoi revoliutsii*, p. 106. Of these, two are pure guesswork and must be discarded (see below).

[2] Aside from the four new districts mentioned above. The results are based on 60 districts (*Vserossiiskoe Uchreditelnoe Sobranie*, p. 210, n. 13, and p. 211, n. 16). The editors accredit 55 districts to Sviatitski though he himself claims only 54. As they present only four new districts (p. xxviii), there are one or two others unaccounted for.

[3] The third column is based on 60 districts. Fifty-two of these are listed in Sviatitski's table, four in the AOR compilation, and four appear for the first time in this study.

Ekaterinoslav, and the Northern Front of the army — it has been possible to produce more complete returns than are found in Sviatitski, the differences resulting from substitution being especially large in the case of Tver, Saratov, Chernigov, Ekaterinoslav, and the Northern Front.[4] On the other hand, it has been necessary to reduce the totals given by Sviatitski through the deletion of two entire districts — Mogilev and the Caucasian Front — where he admits having resorted to pure guesswork in the absence of any returns.[5] The figures for the city of Moscow are cut down to eliminate duplication, since Sviatitski added the garrison vote to totals that already contained it.[6] In a number of other instances more detailed or more accurate returns have been substituted for those contained in his table.[7] On balance, the necessity of taking away from Sviatitski's totals as well as adding to them causes the work of revision appearing in the third column to seem less substantial than actually is the case.

The four new districts (Orenburg, Don, Stavropol, and the Transcaucasus) disclosed by Soviet research add no less than 4,298,854 votes to Sviatitski's total.[8] In the third column these

[4] For example, in the case of Saratov, Sviatitski divides a total of 390,211 votes among the parties, 196,400 for the SR's, 113,592 for the Bolsheviks, etc. Much more complete returns are used in the present study, the total vote being 954,559, of which the SR share was 564,250 and the Bolshevik 225,000. Even so, one *uezd* (Kamyshin) was still out. See the editorial, "Chleny Uchreditelnago Sobraniia ot Saratovskoi gubernii," in *Vestnik Privolzhskago Kraia*, no. 2 (December 16, 1917).

[5] *Itogi vyborov*, p. 25; "Itogi vyborov," *God russkoi revoliutsii*, pp. 106–107. 825,000 votes for Mogilev and 420,000 for the Caucasian Front are thus eliminated.

[6] This becomes apparent from a study and comparison of the accounts in the *Russkiia Vedomosti*, no. 257 (November 24, 1917), the *Russkoe Slovo*, no. 257 (November 24, 1917), and the *Izvestiia Moskovskago Soveta*, no. 213 (November 24, 1917).

[7] So for Vladimir, Moscow province, Kursk, Voronezh, Tambov, Tobolsk, Ienisei, Transbaikal region, Poltava, Kharkov, Taurida, and the Black Sea Fleet. Some of these changes are insignificant but others are substantial (e.g., a reduction of 65,250 in the total vote cast in the Taurida). An error of 20,000 was detected in Sviatitski's figures for the Transbaikal Region.

[8] AOR, *Vserossiiskoe Uchreditelnoe Sobranie*, p. xxviii. Unfortunately, there is no breakdown of the vote save for the SR, Bolshevik, and Kadet

have been included, along with an additional two and a half million votes — 2,569,650 to be exact — which represent the fruits of the present investigation, having been assembled independently either of Sviatitski or of the Archives of the October Revolution.

The table of returns for the whole country reveals clearly the over-all results of the election. Three weeks after the October Revolution, the Bolsheviks had signally failed to secure popular sanction for their seizure of power and had mustered only one-fourth of the electorate behind their banner. No amount of turning and twisting on their part could conceal their discomfiture. On the other hand, the various socialistic parties of all types and description had scored overwhelmingly — more than four-fifths of the people stood behind them, or at any rate had chosen their lists. But what kind of "socialism" was it that had triumphed? Mainly the Narodnik brand, to which the Marxists would deny the very name of socialism.[9] The peasants, as will be shown below, had given their suffrage to the Socialist Revolutionary party, traditionally associated in their minds with immediate expropriation of the land without compensation to the owners; that they themselves were not to have the land as private property meant very little to them, at least for the time being, since they had no concept of property comparable to that which had arisen

---

parties, the one exception being the Menshevik vote in Transcaucasia (*ibid.*, p. 213, n. 20). The Kadet vote for the Don Region is omitted, apparently by mistake. In all probability, however, it represents the discrepancy between the announced total and the sum of the votes for the two lists given plus the unclassified remainder. The Cossack vote is not given for either the Don or Orenburg districts, nor is the large Mohammedan or Armenian vote in the Transcaucasus reported separately. From another source, based on a total of 1,411,500 votes as against the official figure of 1,406,620, we learn that the Don Cossack list received 640,000 votes (45 percent of the total) (V. A. Antonov-Ovseenko, *Zapiski o grazhdanskoi voine*, I [Moscow, 1924], 194). It is apparent that this is approximately the correct figure, and that statements fixing the vote at 900,000 or above are gross exaggerations (see, for example, K. P. Kakliugin, "Voiskovoi Ataman A. M. Kaledin i ego vremia," *Donskaia Letopis*, no. 2 [1923], p. 124).

[9] "Narodnicheskii sotsializm — gnilaia i smerdiashchaia mertvechina" (Narodnik socialism is foul and stinking carrion), wrote Lenin on one occasion ("Chto delaetsia v narodnichestve i chto delaetsia v derevne?" *Sochineniia* (2nd ed.), XVI [1912–13], 312).

in Western lands under the influence of the Roman law.[10] Whether they would have developed a property consciousness once they were in actual possession of the land is, of course, a moot question, but one of sufficient validity to cause the impartial observer to view with skepticism the exultations of Narodnik spokesmen who hailed the election as a grandiose triumph for collectivism.[11]

But if the victory of socialism was inconclusive, what can be said about the showing on the other side, where the adherents of the traditional order of society were gathered under the banner of the Constitutional Democrats and in a number of special interest groups? These people had sustained a dreadful beating at the polls; they had experienced not so much a walloping as a washout. They were not even in the running, for the main fight had taken place within the revolutionary camp, between the Bolshevik wing of the Social Democrats and the SR branch of the Populist movement. It is true that to the figures given under the heading of Russian nonsocialist parties must be added a considerable number of Cossack votes from Orenburg and eastern Siberia, which appear in the residue of 2,151,368 votes in the third column but which are not indicated separately in the sources and hence can only roughly be estimated.[12] Even complete returns from the Cossack districts,

[10] In Russia the principles of the Roman law were too recently established and too restricted in scope to have acquired dominion over the minds of the people. This had been one of the points of departure for the Socialist Revolutionaries in constructing their ideology. See *Protokoly pervago sezda partii sotsialistov-revoliutsionerov* (n.p., 1906), pp. 207, 220–228; "Agrarnaia programma russkoi sotsial-demokratii," *Revoliutsionnaia Rossiia*, no. 40 (January 15, 1904), p. 9; and especially V. M. Chernov, *Zemlia i pravo: Sbornik statei* (Petrograd, 1919), pp. 130–131, 133–134, 167.

[11] So Sviatitski, *Kogo russkii narod izbral svoimi predstaviteliami?*, p. 7, and "Itogi vyborov," *God russkoi revoliutsii*, p. 119.

[12] In Orenburg the SR's got two seats with 110,172 votes and the Bolsheviks three with 163,425; therefore the Orenburg Cossack list must have received in excess of 200,000 votes, since four seats were obtained. Here the residue of 378,511 was swelled by the Bashkir Federalists, who won two places (base figures from AOR, *Vserossiiskoe Uchreditelnoe Sobranie*, p. xxviii; Cossack seats ascertained from list of members of the Constituent Assembly, in *ibid.*, pp. 116–138). Sviatitski assigns 56,050 votes to the Cossacks in eastern Siberia on the basis of partial returns (*Itogi vyborov*, p. 36). As this is a lump sum, undivided by districts, it is necessarily placed in the residue.

The Vote by Parties for the Whole Country

	Sviatitski	AOR	Present Study
RUSSIAN SOCIALIST PARTIES			
SR	16,509,756[a]	17,490,837[b]	15,848,004
SD Bolshevik	9,023,963	9,562,358	9,844,637
SD Menshevik	668,064	1,248,958	1,364,826
Popular Socialist	312,038	?	322,078[c]
Other socialist	211,187	?	183,512
RUSSIAN NONSOCIALIST PARTIES			
Const. Democratic	1,856,639	?	1,986,601
Cossack	79,162	?	663,112
Landowner	215,542	?	171,245
Right .... ⎱	292,133	⎰ ?	109,161
Orthodox .... ⎰		⎱ ?	155,341
Old Believer	73,464	?	53,999
Other Christian	....	?	18,179
Other nonsocialist	....	?	91,381
UKRAINIAN PARTIES			
Ukr. Socialist Bloc	506,887	?	3,556,581
Ukr. SR	3,433,574[d]	3,433,574[d]	1,286,157
Ukr. SD	95,117	?	95,117
Minor groups	....	?	19,212
Total	4,035,578		4,957,067
Joint lists:			
Ukr. SR and SR[e]	....	?	1,203,135
Ukr. SR and Left SR ..	....	?	11,871
Ukr. SR, Ukr. SD, and			
Jewish Socialist	....	?	4,219
Ukr. and Tatar	....	?	53,000
Total	....		1,272,225
MOHAMMEDAN PARTIES			
Mohammedan Nationalist .	576,693	?	484,464
Mohammedan Left and SR	515,272	?	458,272
Total	1,091,965		942,736
OTHER NATIONALITIES			
Armenian Dashnaktsutiun .	....	?	over 350,000
Bashkir	195,230	?	13,100
Buriat	65,403	?	15,464

Chuvash	235,547	?	235,552
Esthonian:			
Nonsocialist	....	?	85,107
Labor	....	?	64,704
SR	....	?	17,726
SD	....	?	9,244
Total	....		176,781
Finnish Socialist	14,000	?	....
German:			
Nationalist	130,579	?	121,614
Socialist	44,507	?	42,156
Total	175,086		163,770
Greek	....	..	9,143
Jewish:			
Nationalist, etc.	550,075	?	417,215
Bund	....	?	31,123
Poalei Zion	....	?	20,538
Other socialist	....	?	29,322
Total	....		498,198
Lettish	67,508	?	69,242
Polish	154,809	?	125,240
White Russian	12,007	?	15,517
Other national	....	?	6,224
Total	....		1,678,231
Nonclassified residue	417,804	?	2,151,368[f]
TOTALS FOR COUNTRY	36,256,960	not given	41,686,876[g]

[a] Includes 1,228,535 votes cast jointly for SR's and Ukrainian SR's and hence inseparable; includes also 1,020,000 votes arbitrarily assigned to Mogilev and the Caucasian Front. Observance of same standards of accuracy as in the third column would cut total without more ado to 14,261,221.

[b] Includes same inaccuracies as above except in case of Mogilev province, for which actual returns were available. This is apparent from study of AOR: *Vserossiiskoe Uchreditelnoe Sobranie*, p. xxviii and p. 210, n. 13.

[c] Includes several joint lists with kindred groups.

[d] Includes civilian districts (e.g., Kiev) where joint list with Ukrainian SD's was presented. Hence inaccurate, though most votes cast for the Ukrainian socialist bloc were undoubtedly SR rather than SD.

[e] Included by Sviatitski in SR total, but inseparable and can not be assigned to either group. See note *a* above.

[f] Includes all votes known to have been cast but not identifiable by party. Of this total 1,167,974 are contributed by the Soviet source. See note 8 in this chapter.

[g] Eliminating duplication of 126,827 votes in Olonets province where special electoral system prevailed. Here there were two seats to be filled and only two candidates, one SR and one Menshevik, each voter having two votes.

however, would not raise the total conservative vote above 3,500,000 out of a grand total of nearly 42,000,000.

These figures tell us a great deal. They reveal in stark outline certain of the fundamental weaknesses of Old Russia: the numerical insignificance of the middle class, the loss of vitality of once powerful institutions like the monarchy and the church, and the absence of a strong national consciousness such as had come to the rescue of Western conservatism when the old mainstays of monarchism and clericalism began to give way. One can only marvel at the eclipse of clerical influence, at the miserable showing not only of the Orthodox candidates but also of the Old Believers, who between them could not muster a quarter of a million followers at the polls. Except in the Mohammedan communities of the east, the priesthood had ceased to be an important political factor. The support of the extreme right overlapped that of the clergy but was equally ineffective; only in Nizhni Novgorod province did their combined forces make a real showing.[13] It seems ironical that the landowners' ticket, the prospects of which could not conceivably have been darker than in November of 1917, should have drawn more votes on the conservative side than any other save only the Kadet and the Cossack.

The weakness of Great Russian nationalism contrasts markedly with the spirit of lesser ethnic groups, now released from the restraints imposed by tsarism and asserting their separate identity — often, it would seem, with more vigor than validity. The five million votes obtained in the clear by the various Ukrainian lists constitute an impressive showing from any point of view, and must be augmented by at least another half million votes as the Ukrainian share of the joint lists agreed on with other parties. However one may estimate the strength of Ukrainian separatism,

[13] The list headed by Archbishop Sergius received 48,428 votes out of a total of 579,897. One source speaks of it as the Faith and Fatherland list; another, as the Christian Union (*Izvestiia Vserossiiskoi po delam o vyborakh v Uchreditelnoe Sobranie Komissii*, no. 24 [December 16, 1917], p. 4; AOR, *Vserossiiskoe Uchreditelnoe Sobranie*, p. 137). In column 3 it appears under Orthodox.

no one can deny that Little Russian particularism had real force behind it. The reverse is true in White Russia, where it is scarcely possible to speak of a particularistic consciousness in the light of the wholly negligible quantity of votes cast for White Russian lists in Vitebsk and Minsk provinces and on the Western Front.

About a million votes had gone to Mohammedan lists, either to those regarded as leftist because of a tinge of Narodnik socialism, or to those ranked as conservative because of a nationalist label. This convincing demonstration of strength in itself becomes still more impressive when the origin of the votes is considered, for nearly all of them were amassed along the Volga or in the Ural region, without reference to the great Mohammedan stronghold of Central Asia, where no election was held,[14] or to the Transcaucasus, for which no separate returns are available.[15] Since in the Urals and along the Volga the Mohammedan confession and Tatar nationality are virtually synonymous, and since here the Tatars have been engulfed by the tide of Russian expansion and their identity endangered, it is proper to regard this vote as more a tribute to Tatar nationalism than to the Prophet's cult. List designations, in fact, bear this out with headings such as "Musulman National Council" or "Musulman National Committee." As conclusive proof, it may be pointed out that the Bashkirs, who

[14] Such, at any rate, is the commonly accepted version. See Vishniak, *Vserossiiskoe Uchreditelnoe Sobranie*, pp. 91–92. Sviatitski's table contains no returns from Central Asia. However, in another article he lists an SR member from the Fergana district of Turkestan. See "Fraktsiia partii S.-R. Uchreditelnago Sobraniia i eia deiatelnost," *Partiinyia Izvestiia*, no. 5 (Jan. 20, 1918), pp. 32–36. A strange contradiction is to be noted in the Soviet study: in the foreword to the list of members of the Constituent Assembly the editors state that there were none from Fergana (AOR, *Vserossiiskoe Uchreditelnoe Sobranie*, p. 115), and then in the list itself they proceed to give no less than five delegates from Fergana, including the one mentioned by Sviatitski (*ibid.*, pp. 134, 137, 138).

[15] The Mohammedan vote in the Transcaucasus is lumped with many others in the general residue of 2,151,368. Though the vote itself cannot be ascertained, the deputies returned can be picked out from the general list. There were twelve of them, of whom seven were elected on the main list, the Musulman National Committee and the Musavat party (*ibid.*, pp. 116ff). Since the Mensheviks in the Transcaucasus secured 14 seats with 569,362 votes, the total Mohammedan vote must have been about half a million.

likewise are Mohammedans, ran their own candidates on separate lists in competition with their Tatar co-religionists.[16]

Of the non-Moslem ethnic groups in the east of Russia only the Chuvash, with their quarter of a million votes, made any considerable showing. Finnish tribes like the Mordvins and Cheremis were either too inert or too nearly assimilated to seek political expression apart from the main Russian parties.[17]

In general it can be said that the provinces on the periphery of Russia, northwest, west, south, and east, yielded a very large contingent of votes for the national minorities. In many-peopled Transcaucasia there was an impressive turnout in the case of the Armenians, whose revolutionary organization, the Dashnaktsutiun, secured ten seats in the Constituent Assembly.[18] Where German or Polish elements formed a substantial part of the population, their own national lists were favored. The Jews, as might be expected, proved to be a highly articulate group, with many of their voters preferring some specifically Jewish list to those of the big supernational parties. The Lettish and Esthonian vote, though considerable, was much less than it could have been, partly because of the German occupation of Courland and Riga, but mainly because of the great strength displayed in the Baltic provinces by the local SD affiliate of Bolshevism.

In respect to the apportionment of seats in the Constituent Assembly, the Archives of the October Revolution have painstakingly assembled a list of 707 deputies, divided into the following partisan groupings: [19]

---

[16] Bashkir lists were offered in Samara, Perm, Ufa, and Orenburg provinces. Two deputies were elected from Orenburg, two from Ufa, and one from Perm (*ibid.*). Sviatitski credits the Bashkirs with 195,230 votes ("Itogi vyborov," *God russkoi revoliutsii*, p. 119), but he had no returns from Orenburg. This writer does not have the figures by districts save for Samara, where the vote was negligible (13,100).

[17] In Viatka the Cheremis did have a joint list with the Popular Socialists.

[18] As singled out from the list of members in AOR, *Vserossiiskoe Uchreditelnoe Sobranie*, pp. 116ff. The figure of 350,000, taken from the *Delo Naroda*, no. 228 (December 9, 1917), and given in the table above, constituted the bulk of the Armenian vote but apparently was still not definitive.

[19] AOR, *Vserossiiskoe Uchreditelnoe Sobranie*, p. 115. The editors concede that on the basis of existing records it is not possible to determine with

```
SR's ..................... 370
Left SR's [20] ............. 40
Bolsheviks .............. 175
Mensheviks ............. 16
Popular Socialists ......... 2
Kadets ................. 17
National groups .......... 86
Unknown ............... 1
```

A more detailed classification is given by Sviatitski on the basis of virtually the same number of deputies, elected as of the middle of January 1918.[21] For purposes of comparison, the same combinations are indicated in the second column as are employed in the foregoing tabulation.

```
SR's proper .............. 299 ⎫
                               ⎬ 380
Ukrainian SR's [22] ......... 81 ⎭
Left SR's ............... 39
Bolsheviks .............. 168
Mensheviks ............. 18
Popular Socialists ......... 4
Constitutional Democrats ... 15 ⎫
                               ⎬ 17
Rightists ................ 2 ⎭
Musulmans, Bashkirs, Kirghiz 28 ⎤
Armenians ............... 10 ⎥
Jews, Poles, Letts, Esthonians 9 ⎥
National SR groups [23] ..... 19 ⎬ 77
Ukrainian SD's ........... 2 ⎥
Cossacks ............... 9 ⎦
        Total ................. 703
```

exactitude the party affiliation of the deputies; they claim only to have made a fair approximation in submitting these figures. The editors were much more concerned with compiling the list of members (pp. 116–138) than with compiling the numerical results and consequently did a much better job.

[20] Schism in PSR developed after election was held. See p. 72.

[21] *Kogo russkii narod izbral svoimi predstaviteliami?*, pp. 10–11. The author places the total number of seats to be filled at 817. The Soviet study (p. 115) mentions 815; the number of seats allotted to each civilian district is given in the table, pp. 140–142. The hundred-odd deputies who do not figure in the above tabulations were never chosen. See above, pp. 6, 19.

[22] The Soviet study (p. 213, n. 21) mentions 69 Ukrainian SR's as elected in nine civilian districts. The number elected at the front is not given.

[23] Musulman, Chuvash, Moldavian, and Buriat.

It is not possible to go beyond these tabulations, as they contain the full complement of deputies elected in districts for which neither Sviatitski nor the Archives of the October Revolution could produce the actual returns (for example, Kaluga, Bessarabia, Podolia, Olonets, Baltic Fleet, Esthonia). They may be considered, therefore, as substantially complete.

CHAPTER III

ANALYSIS OF RETURNS FOR REPRESENTATIVE DISTRICTS

So MUCH for a general survey of the results of the election, based on the country-wide totals for each party. In so vast and varied a land as Russia, however, it is necessary to do more than present a general survey, and not so much for the sake of completeness as for clarity and comprehension. Only a more detailed inspection can reveal significant features of the election, for Russia is no compact nation-state but rather a spacious empire, in which factors of class, location, and nationality are all involved in varying proportions. Country-wide totals, therefore, are not simply a projection of more or less uniform local results but rather a composite of regional returns which often are sharply at variance with one another. Nor is this difference induced solely by diversity of race and religion; the behavior of the same class of the same nationality may vary from region to region, as was notably true of the Great Russian peasantry in the central region around Moscow and in the black-earth zone to the south and southeast. In these two regions difference in soil gave rise to a different economic setup, and this in turn united with other factors to produce a different political outlook.

A number of electoral districts, therefore, have been singled out for closer inspection and analysis, each being representative of a certain region and free from defects in the statistical sense. Let us begin with the northwestern or lake region and proceed through Great Russia in an easterly and southeasterly direction, reserving other portions of the empire for later analysis.

Among the four provinces in the lake region, Novgorod is the most suitable. The election results there are given in the accompanying table.[1]

---

[1] *Delo Naroda*, no. 228 (December 9, 1917); *Pravda*, no. 205 (December 3, 1917). Figures are unofficial.

Lake or Northwestern Region: Novgorod Province

SR	220,665
Bolshevik	203,658
Kadet	31,480
Menshevik	9,336
Popular Socialist	10,314
Landowner	7,804
House-owner	1,178
Coöperative	1,123
Unity (Plekhanov)	860
Total	486,418

Here the contest lay between the Socialist Revolutionaries and the Bolsheviks, the Kadets trailing far behind. Novgorod was not an industrial province; how, then, could a Marxist party fare so well in a rural constituency? The answer is to be found in the close economic ties between the Novgorod peasantry and the working class of St. Petersburg, whither many inhabitants of other provinces — and particularly of Novgorod — [2] were accustomed to repair in search of seasonal employment without, however, surrendering their peasant status at home. This half-proletarian, half-peasant type was a common phenomenon in northern Russia, and its prevalence goes far to explain why, in 1917, Bolshevism should have spread with such rapidity from industrial centers into the surrounding countryside. If the peasant did not have a share in industry himself, he was likely to have family connections with the proletariat, itself still raw and green, and but one step removed from the soil.

The influence of the town on the country is still more pronounced in the central industrial region, where peasants were drawn not only to both metropolises but also to the lesser industrial centers of their own provinces. Vladimir, with its many textile mills at Ivanovo-Voznesensk and elsewhere, was the most extensively industrialized province in the region, aside from Mos-

[2] *Rossiia: Polnoe geograficheskoe opisanie nashego otechestva*, ed. V. P. Semenov (St. Petersburg: A. F. Devrien, 1899–1914), Vol. III, *Ozernaia Oblast*, p. 206.

cow itself. Here Bolshevism had always commanded a following, and by the fall of 1917 virtually the entire proletariat had rallied to Lenin's standard, turning its back on Menshevism and pulling a large part of the peasantry away from the Socialist Revolutionaries. As a consequence, the Bolsheviks achieved an absolute majority in the balloting for the Constituent Assembly, as shown in the accompanying tabulation.[3]

Central Industrial Region: Vladimir Province

SR	197,311
Bolshevik	337,941
Kadet	38,035
Menshevik	13,074
Popular Socialist	6,908
Coöperative	1,482
Right ("Regeneration")	9,209
Total	603,960

Again, we have a duel between two parties. But this time the tables are turned, for in Vladimir there is a numerous and strong-willed proletariat, as there was not in Novgorod, and many of the peasants are drawn along in its wake. Of the thirteen *uezds* into which the province was divided, only two were carried by the SR's, and these were precisely the most remote and the least developed industrially.[4] Rarely can so perfect a correlation between political, geographical, and economic factors be found. The Constitutional Democrats are no stronger here than in Novgorod, polling only 6.3 per cent of the total vote; the Mensheviks fare very badly;

[3] N. Shakhanov, *1917-yi god vo Vladimirskoi gubernii: Khronika sobytii* (Vladimir, 1927), pp. 128–130, 139, quoting from the local press. Figures are complete but unofficial. Other sources (including Sviatitski) differ slightly, but are based on earlier returns and hence are rejected.

[4] They gained a plurality (42.4 per cent) in Viazniki *uezd*, which lay to the east of the industrial belt but had some linen and hemp weaving, and won decisively (57.4 per cent of the vote) in Gorokhovets *uezd*, situated still further to the east and containing no factories whatever (according to the census of 1897) (*Rossiia: Polnoe geograficheskoe opisanie*, Vol. I, *Moskovskaia promyshlennaia oblast i Verkhnee Povolzhe*, pp. 86, 312–313; electoral figures from Shakhanov).

there are some Popular Socialists in Vladimir as in Novgorod, but not many; the members of the coöperative societies, and even their employees, obviously do not share the desire of a few high functionaries like Berkenheim to bring the movement into politics; [5] a group of reactionaries comes out into the open and bids for support, but elicits only a weak response from the electorate (1.5 per cent of the whole).

These results in what for Russia was a highly industrialized district stand in glaring contrast to those in a typical black-earth province like Kursk.[6]

Black-Earth Region: Kursk Province

SR	868,743
Bolshevik	119,127
Kadet	47,199
Menshevik	6,037
Popular Socialist	8,594
Landowner	8,656
Total	1,058,356

In Kursk there was little besides farming, and peasants were really peasants. The influence of the metropolitan centers was weak. As a consequence, the SR vote shoots upward and the Bolshevik vote drops precipitously, the ratio being better than 7:1. Even so, Lenin's party still occupies second place with more than 100,000 votes, relatively few of which could be proletarian. How, then, were they obtained? The answer is that soldiers — either those from rear garrisons or those coming back from the front — everywhere conducted a fierce agitation on behalf of Bolshevism and disposed numbers of peasants in favor of a party which otherwise they almost certainly would have passed up.[7] Thus was Bolshe-

---

[5] Sviatitski, as a good SR, celebrates the fiasco of the coöperatives at the polls, since their political venture could have succeeded only at the cost of his party ("Itogi vyborov," *God russkoi revoliutsii*, p. 118).

[6] *Izvestiia Vserossiiskoi po delam o vyborakh v Uchreditelnoe Sobranie Komissii*, no. 24 (December 16, 1917), p. 3. Returns are complete and official — a rare occurrence.

[7] This phenomenon will be discussed in Chapters IV and V.

vism sustained in districts with little or no industry. The Kadets are as weak here as elsewhere, the Mensheviks even weaker, while the Popular Socialists continue steady in their insignificance. The right is represented in Kursk by a landowners' list, which gets the votes of . . . landowners. One notes the simplicity of the electoral pattern in Kursk — despite the presence of a large Little Russian element [8] in the southern *uezds*, it is a remarkably homogeneous province in every sense of the word.

The same cannot be said of the provinces in the Kama-Ural region, the next that claims our attention. Ethnographical diversity is reflected in a more complex table than hitherto.[9]

Kama-Ural Region: Kazañ Province

SR	260,000
Bolshevik	50,000
Kadet	32,000
Menshevik	4,906
Coöperative and Independent Socialist	2,993
Orthodox	12,000
Bourgeois splinter	2,000
Right SR's	10,000
Mohammedan Socialists	153,151
Mohammedan Nationalists	100,000
Chuvash	226,496
Residue	5,050
Total	858,596

There is a large Chuvash vote — claimed by the SR's [10] — and a

---

[8] 580,000 by the census of 1897. The Little Russians, however, had not retained their purity of type and had mixed to a considerable extent with their Great Russian neighbors (*Rossiia: Polnoe geograficheskoe opisanie*, Vol. II, *Srednerusskaia chernozëmnaia oblast*, pp. 168–169).

[9] *Russkiia Vedomosti*, no. 277 (December 29, 1917). The round numbers, of course, indicate approximate figures only. For a number of reasons it would have been better to take Perm or Ufa instead of Kazañ, but no returns are available except those in Sviatitski, and he does not give a complete breakdown by parties.

[10] Sviatitski, "Itogi vyborov," *God russkoi revoliutsii*, p. 112, and *Kogo russkii narod izbral svoimi predstaviteliami?*, p. 4. But the list was a com-

large Tatar (Mohammedan) vote, divided between left and right in the ratio of 3:2. The bulk of the Russian population again prefers the PSR, while the Kadets and Mensheviks betray their customary weakness. But Bolshevism, also, is weak in Kazañ — a surprising circumstance in view of the outstanding military significance of the city and district and the fact that Kazañ was the station of one of the largest interior garrisons in the country.[11] The explanation probably lies both in the presence of a large native element, much less responsive to Bolshevik propaganda than the Russians themselves, and in the special conditions within the SR organization, which in Kazañ province had fallen under the domination of its left wing, the violent and semi-anarchistic preachings of which afforded a thoroughly radical alternative to Bolshevism. Hence the local schism in the PSR and the attempt of the right wing to run its own ticket, which ended in fiasco.[12] The 12,000 votes cast under the banner of Orthodoxy show that the political influence of the clergy was as little marked here as elsewhere, despite the presence of a rival faith, which presumably should have sharpened religious loyalties.

Proceeding now across the Urals into western Siberia, we encounter once more, as in the case of the black-earth zone, an electoral pattern that is simple and clear: [13]

---

posite one and was designated as that of the "General Chuvash National Congress, Chuvash Military Committee, and Chuvash PSR." See under Gavriil F. Aliunov, deputy from Kazañ, in the list of members of the Constituent Assembly, AOR, *Vserossiiskoe Uchreditelnoe Sobranie*, p. 116.

[11] N. Ezhov, *Voennaia Kazañ v 1917g. Kratkii otchet* (Kazañ, 1927), pp. 6–8. Soldiers everywhere were notoriously susceptible to Bolshevik blandishments. The Kazañ military district embraced a vast territory (10 provinces and 2 regions), the administration of which centered in the city.

[12] In general the SR voters went for the label without bothering to find out whether it covered a leftist or centrist or rightist selection of candidates. It all depended on which faction controlled the provincial organization and drew up the list. Dissident tickets, whether of the left or right, were regularly voted down.

[13] Sviatitski, *Itogi vyborov*, pp. 34–36. Sviatitski ascribes to Tomsk 8,048 votes cast for a German list, but it is clear from his own figures that these votes should have been included in the returns from the Altai district instead of from Tomsk.

Siberia: Tomsk Province

SR	541,153
Bolshevik	51,456
Kadet	18,618
Menshevik	5,769
Popular Socialist	15,802
Coöperative	2,686
Total	635,484

Here in territory where neither the influence of the large cities nor of the front was felt at first-hand, the SR's had swept the field, polling 85 per cent of the vote and increasing the ratio between themselves and the second-place Bolsheviks even beyond what it had been for the black-earth province of Kursk. The other parties hardly figure at all: the Popular Socialists, though stronger here than elsewhere, still fall wide of electing a single deputy. In eastern Siberia, with its mining districts and substantial labor movement, the Bolsheviks did somewhat better and the SR victory was less one-sided,[14] but the population here was thinner, so that, taken as a whole, Siberia gave the SR's a larger percentage of votes than any other region.[15]

Turning from a survey of the regions of Great Russia to Little Russia, we encounter the most complex electoral pattern of any yet examined. The most purely Ukrainian of all parts of the Ukraine is Poltava province,[16] and, as fate would have it, the election returns from there are complete and official — a welcome exception to the rule. They afford, therefore, an excellent insight into the distribution of strength in the Ukraine: [17]

[14] In the Ienisei district, for example, the SR's received 229,671 votes against 96,138 for the Bolsheviks (*Izvestiia Vserossiiskoi po delam o vyborakh v Uchreditelnoe Sobranie Komissii*, no. 24 [December 16, 1917], p. 3).

[15] Lenin, "Vybory v Uchreditelnoe Sobranie i diktatura proletariata," *Sochineniia* (2nd ed.), XXIV, 632, where the figure is given as 75 per cent, based on the statistics of Sviatitski.

[16] 97.6 per cent of the population was Little Russian in 1897 (*Rossiia: Polnoe geograficheskoe opisanie*, Vol. VII, *Malorossiia*, p. 98).

[17] *Izvestiia Vserossiiskoi po delam o vyborakh v Uchreditelnoe Sobranie Komissii*, no. 24 (December 16, 1917), pp. 4, 7.

Little Russia: Poltava Province

SR and Ukrainian SR (joint list)	198,437
Bolshevik	64,460
Kadet	18,105
Menshevik and Jewish Bund	5,993
Popular Socialist and Coöperatives	4,391
Landowner	61,115
Ukrainian SR	727,247
Ukrainian SD	22,613
Ukrainian Socialist Federalist	9,092
Ukrainian National Republican	1,070
Jewish National Committee	13,722
Jewish list	12,100
Jewish People's Party	6,448
Jewish Socialist Workers' Party	1,482
Poalei Zion	879
Local peasants' soviet	445
List without title	1,657
Total	1,149,256

No other district presents more interesting or more revealing figures. The one thing that stands out most clearly is the strength of Ukrainian sentiment. The voters in Poltava province were confronted with two lists — one offered by the Ukrainian SR's standing alone, the other in combination with the All-Russian SR party, here dominated by its left wing and hence prepared to go the limit in meeting autonomist demands. Either list would have afforded an outlet to nationalist sentiment, yet the voters chose the simon-pure Ukrainian SR list in the ratio of 7:2. In the face of such a clear-cut demonstration of strength, it is simply not possible to contend that the Ukrainian movement was a weak and artificial thing, concocted by a group of hyper-nationalistic intellectuals; yet it would also be inadmissible to contend that the returns indicate a desire for separation from Russia. If the assertion of the Great Russian chauvinists is definitely disproved, the claim of the Little Russian separatists is not substantiated. What happened was that the Little Russian peasantry followed the lead of the intellectuals in an impressive manifestation of devotion to their folkways without by any means implying that they desired the independent statehood toward which the intellectuals were steadily gravitating. There is no reason to assume that the peasant voters would not have been satisfied with autonomy within the framework of a federal state, even though the intellectuals who led them might not have been. Little Russian particularism is not necessarily identical with Ukrainian separatism.

In keeping with the almost exclusively agrarian character of the Ukrainian people, it will be noted that the other Ukrainian parties polled scarcely any votes at all, the Ukrainian SD's having less than one-thirtieth the strength of their agrarian rivals. The parties of All-Russian significance attracted little strength in Poltava province: Bolshevism was weak here, but not nearly so weak as Menshevism; among the conservative groups, the Kadets with their Great Russian bias were quite outdistanced in this opulent farming region by the landowners' list, which did better here than anywhere else in the country.[18]

Quite different is the picture in White Russia, where Vitebsk province may be taken as indicative of the general trend.[19] Two

White Russia: Vitebsk Province

SR	150,279
Bolshevik	287,101
Kadet	8,132
Menshevik and Bund	12,471
Popular Socialist	3,599
Landowner	6,098
Peasants' list	9,752
White Russian	9,019
Lettish Socialist Federalist	26,990
Lettish Nationalist	5,881
Letgallian Nationalist	5,118
Jewish Nationalist	24,790
Polish Nationalist	10,556
Splinter	752
Total	560,538

[18] Regarding the nature of this party in the Ukraine, see Chapter IV, note 18.

[19] *Delo Naroda*, no. 220 (November 30, 1917). This source gives the total as 560,540.

features stand out from these returns: the weakness of White
Russian particularism and the strength of Bolshevism. Whether
because there was less to build on or because the intellectuals were
slower in getting started, the White Russian movement was only
a tiny trickle compared to the broad stream of Ukrainian nationalism, and was quite overshadowed in voting strength by the
minority groups of Letts, Poles, and Jews. Aside from these, the
population had been content to divide its suffrage among the parties of All-Russian significance, and almost exclusively between
the Bolsheviks and the SR's, the former having decidedly the
upper hand in this province. There is no satisfactory explanation
of the fact that the Bolsheviks inflicted a stinging defeat on the
SR's in two White Russian provinces — Vitebsk and Minsk [20] —
only themselves to sustain a rout in a third province, Mogilev.[21]
The influence of the front with its milling mob of Bolshevized
soldiers was no doubt of great moment in Vitebsk and Minsk,[22]
but such influence must also have extended to Mogilev province —
after all, general headquarters was at Mogilev on the Dnieper.[23]
The provinces of Vitebsk and Minsk resemble those of the central
industrial region in that only in these parts of the country did

[20] In Vitebsk province, the SR vote was 27 per cent of the total (see table
above); in Minsk province, 20 per cent of the total (computed from figures
in *Izvestiia Vserossiiskoi po delam o vyborakh v Uchreditelnoe Sobranie
Komissii*, no. 24 [December 16, 1917], pp. 3–4).

[21] As previously stated, no valid returns have ever been published for
this district. But the SR vote was 70 per cent of the total (AOR, *Vserossiiskoe Uchreditelnoe Sobranie*, p. 210, n. 13). Twelve SR's were elected from
Mogilev province, as against only one Bolshevik and two Jewish deputies.
See report in Sviatitski, "Fraktsiia partii S.-R. Uchreditelnago Sobraniia i
eia deiatelnost," *Partiinyia Izvestiia*, no. 5, pp. 32–36.

[22] *Novaia Zhizn*, no. 201 (December 14, 1917); V. Knorin, *Revoliutsiia i
kontr-revoliutsiia v Belorussii (fevral 1917–fevral 1918)*, Part I (Smolensk,
1920), pp. 58, 61, 63. The Minsk correspondent of Gorki's paper states that
war weariness was at its maximum close to the front. Minsk was closer than
Mogilev, it is true, but the difference in proximity would hardly account for
the phenomenon in question.

[23] Of possible influence on the election was the very great popularity
enjoyed by the SR head of the Mogilev provincial soviet of peasants'
deputies. See N. Ia. Bykhovski, *Vserossiiskii sovet krestianskikh deputatov
1917g.* (Moscow, 1929), p. 170.

the peasantry favor the Bolsheviks over the SR's. One difference, however, was that the Kadet party, weak everywhere, virtually did not exist in White Russia.

For the non-Russian portions of the empire there are satisfactory returns only in the case of the Baltic Provinces, and even there one province — Courland — was eliminated by German conquest and another — Livonia — was partially occupied. The choice is thus narrowed to Esthonia, the returns for which are presented in the accompanying table.[24]

Baltic Provinces: Esthonia

SR	3,200
Bolshevik	119,863
Esthonian SR	17,726
Esthonian SD	9,244
Esthonian Laborite	64,704
Esthonian Democratic	68,085
Esthonian Land Union	17,022
Total	299,844

The field is divided between Bolshevism and Esthonian nationalism, expressed in groupings of varied economic appeal. In this land of Western culture and highly developed social forms there flourished a powerful labor movement, deep red in hue and recruited from workers on large estates as well as from factory hands.[25] The movement was closely connected with Lenin's party through a common bond of internationalism, the weakness of which in the case of other Russian parties had kept them from gaining a foothold in the Baltic Provinces. In Livonia the strength of Bolshevism was truly formidable,[26] greater than anywhere else

---

[24] *Pravda*, no. 206 (December 5, 1917).

[25] A great proportion of the land was in the form of estates, and the estates were individually of unusual size, much above the average for the empire as a whole.

[26] 97,781 votes of a total of 136,080, or 72 per cent, were cast for the SD's of Latvia, the Baltic affiliate of Bolshevism (*Izvestiia Vserossiiskoi po delam o vyborakh v Uchreditelnoe Sobranie Komissii*, no. 24 [December 16, 1917], p. 1).

in the empire, and the support came from the farm hands rather than the city workers, as is seen from the fact that Riga had been taken by the Germans in September and so had been removed from the scope of the election.[27]

There remain two special types of voting districts, the urban and the military. The great metropolitan centers of European Russia — there were only two in this peasant empire — had been constituted as districts in their own right, so that their political complexion is readily apparent from the returns presented in the accompanying table.[28]

	Petrograd City	*Moscow City*
SR	152,230	62,260
Bolshevik	424,027	366,148
Constitutional Democrat	246,506	263,859
Menshevik [29]	29,167	21,597
Popular Socialist	19,109	2,508
Democratic Socialist Bloc	....	35,305
Plekhanov Unity	1,823	....
Orthodox	24,139	....
Roman Catholic	14,382	....
Other religious	3,797	....
Cossack	6,712	....
Residue [30]	15,809	13,086
Total	942,333	764,763

Here the duel of the extremities is the oustanding feature of the election. Here alone in all of Russia did the Constitutional

[27] In the Vollmar district the Bolshevik vote in the town was not only absolutely but also proportionately less than in the surrounding countryside — 73 per cent in the town as against 77 per cent in the *uezd* (*Izvestiia Tsentralnago Ispolnitelnago Komiteta i petrogradskago soveta rabochikh i soldatskikh deputatov*, no. 232 [November 22, 1917], p. 7).

[28] Returns for Petrograd in *Delo Naroda*, no. 211 (November 16, 1917), revised in no. 212 (November 17, 1917); returns for Moscow in *Russkiia Vedomosti*, no. 257 (November 24, 1917).

[29] Schism resulted in two lists in each city: SD (United) and SD (Internationalist). Combined vote given here.

[30] Includes 5,310 votes for a feminist list and 4,696 for the right SR's in the case of Petrograd; includes 4,085 votes for a non-partisan list (probably rightist) in Moscow.

Democrats make a real showing. The election reveals, paradoxically, that the great strongholds of Bolshevism were also the strongholds of the class enemy, for the proletariat was complemented by a numerous bourgeoisie in these centers of business life, and the bourgeoisie was reinforced by government functionaries who staffed the bureaus of the capital and the second administrative center of the empire. These civil servants were rabid against the Bolsheviks, regarding them as enemies of the Russian state. Political consciousness was more highly developed in the big cities than elsewhere and class lines more tightly drawn, the social cleavage being especially marked in the case of Moscow, where almost nothing had been left in between to mitigate the clash of extremes. The SR organization in Petrograd, controlled since September by the left wing of the party,[31] still retained a considerable portion of the following which had made it the strongest party in the capital as recently as the preceding August,[32] but in Moscow the organization had gone to pieces and its support had drained off in two directions, much of it going to the Kadets but more to the Bolsheviks.[33] Finally, it will be noted that in Petrograd the attempt of the extreme right to rally support under a religious banner had ended in failure; virtually the entire nonsocialist electorate, regardless of political shading, had given its suffrage to the Constitutional Democratic party, among whose adherents on this occasion there were no doubt many who were neither constitutionalists nor democrats.[34]

The great, swollen army of Russia, with its millions of reluctant soldiers, had been granted the suffrage. To have withheld it would have meant attainting the election, so large was the segment of population that had been drawn into the war. Each of the five main fronts had been constituted an electoral district, and two more were provided for the sailors, one for the Baltic and one

[31] Control had been wrested from the hands of the centrist faction at the VII city conference (*Delo Naroda*, no. 152, September 12, 1917).

[32] As demonstrated by the municipal election of August 20.

[33] There had been a catastrophic falling off in the SR vote, from 374,885 in the municipal election in June to 62,260 in November. See pp. 52–53.

[34] See Chapter VI, note 9.

for the Black Sea Fleet. The voting at the front and in the navy seems to have been determined by one circumstance alone — the extent to which Bolshevik agitation had been carried on among the rank and file. If the district were remote from the metropolitan centers, and specifically from the influence of the Petrograd Soviet and the Bolshevik party organization, the SR's carried the day, and the farther removed the district was, the greater their degree of success; but on the Northern and Western Fronts the old-line agrarian appeal of the PSR had been overbalanced by intensive propaganda in favor of immediate peace and immediate seizure of the estates, so that here the SR's sustained a crushing defeat and Lenin's party won a great victory.[35] The contrast is seen in the accompanying tabulation.[36]

	Western Front	Roumanian Front
SR	180,582	679,471
Bolshevik	653,430	167,000
Constitutional Democrat	16,750	21,438
Menshevik	8,000	33,858
Ukrainian Socialist Bloc	85,062	180,576
Residue [37]	32,176	46,257
Total	976,000	1,128,600

The observer can only wonder whether the Roumanian Front would have differed from the Western had it not been more insulated against the Bolshevik contagion. Certainly the facts point in that direction. Between the two fronts lay the Southwestern,

[35] For comment of Lenin himself, see "Vybory v Uchreditelnoe Sobranie i diktatura proletariata," *Sochineniia* (2nd ed.), XXIV, 638.

[36] Figures are from Sviatitski's table; it has not been possible to improve on them. In the case of the Northern Front alone has the author of the present study succeeded in locating the complete and official returns. The Western and Roumanian fronts are used here because of the sharpness of the contrast involved.

[37] An earlier tabulation for the Western Front, based on a total of 544,034 votes, gave 15,113 for the Mohammedan Socialists, 3,510 for the White Russians, 3,055 for the Russian Democrats, and 2,429 for the joint Popular Socialist–Plekhanov Unity list (*Izvestiia Tsentralnago Ispolnitelnago Komiteta i petrogradskago soveta*, no. 248 [December 10, 1917], p. 4).

and here the SR's were already stronger than their rivals, though only by a ratio of 4:3. On the other hand, the Caucasian Front was even more remote than the Roumanian, and it was precisely here that the SR's displayed their greatest strength, electing five deputies against one for the Bolsheviks on the basis of incomplete returns.[38] The explanation of their success is simple: the SR leadership of the soldiers' soviets, strongly in favor of national defense, had used its authority to throttle Bolshevik agitation on the front, even denying to that party representation on electoral information committees,[39] and had gotten away with its one-sided policy because of remoteness from the hearth of revolution. Thus the strength of Bolshevism steadily wanes as the influence of the metropolitan centers recedes.[40] Not only the SR's but also the Mensheviks were helped by distance: thus on the Western Front Menshevism was already virtually extinct by the time of the election, whereas on the Roumanian Front it still retained a following, albeit a modest one. The figures presented above show that Constitutional Democracy had no appeal for the rank and file of the troops — few besides the officers could have chosen its list. On the other hand, the figures reveal that the Ukrainian movement had achieved a not inconsiderable following at the front, where leaders like Simon Petliura, deputy from the Roumanian Front, bore the standard ostensibly of Ukrainian socialism, but actually of Ukrainian nationalism.

We have now completed our survey of representative electoral

[38] Sviatitski, "Fraktsiia partii S.-R.," *Partiinyia Izvestiia*, no. 5; confirmed by a search of the list of members in AOR, *Vserossiiskoe Uchreditelnoe Sobranie*, pp. 116–138. Sviatitski gives the number of SR deputies as six in his table in the *God russkoi revoliutsii*, but this must be rejected in favor of the above. As previously stated, no returns are available for the Caucasian Front.

[39] *Revoliutsiia 1917 goda v Azerbaidzhane (khronika sobytii)*, ed. S.Belenky and A. Manvelov (Baku, 1927), pp. 124, 159; *Revoliutsiia 1917 goda v Zakavkazi (Dokumenty, Materialy)*, ed. S. E. Sef (Tiflis, 1927), pp. 84–86, 221–222, 272, 345.

[40] The same is true of the navy. The Bolsheviks overwhelmed the SR's 3 to 1 in the Baltic Fleet, only themselves to succumb by a margin of 2 to 1 in the Black Sea Fleet.

districts. Certain conclusions come readily to mind. The Bolsheviks had the center of the country — the big cities, the industrial towns, and the garrisons of the rear; they controlled those sections of the army most strategically located with reference to Moscow and Petrograd; they even commanded a strong following among the peasants of the central, White Russian, and northwestern regions. The Socialist Revolutionaries had the black-earth zone, the valley of the Volga, and Siberia; in general they were still the peasants' party, though serious defections had taken place. Particularist or separatist movements had strength in the Ukraine, along the Baltic, between the Volga and the Urals, and in the Transcaucasus; of these movements by all odds the most robust was Ukrainian nationalism. Menshevism was a spent force everywhere save in the Transcaucasus, where it was entwined with Georgian nationalism. Constitutional Democracy, for all the support that wealth and position, education and publicity could lend, had been drowned in the mass vote of peasants, soldiers, and workers. Only in Petrograd and Moscow had it marshaled real force. Even so, there was no other grouping on the conservative side that could match such little strength as the Constitutional Democrats possessed. P. N. Durnovo's prophecy had been borne out: the advocates of western constitutionalism were without roots in the Russian people.[41]

Such, broadly speaking, were the results of the election to the Constituent Assembly, expressed in terms of regional geography. They foreshadowed the distribution of strength and the territorial complexion of the approaching civil war. The deep significance of the election in this respect was not lost on Lenin, despite the

[41] "Zapiska," *Krasnaia Nov*, no. 6/10 (November–December 1922), pp. 195–197 (full text, pp. 182–199); English translation in F. A. Golder, *Documents of Russian History 1914–1917* (New York and London, 1927), pp. 3–23, pertinent passages pp. 19–22. This celebrated memorandum, unbelievably accurate in its prognostications, was laid before the Emperor Nicholas II in February 1914. Nothing is more indicative of the hopeless condition of the monarchy than its failure to turn to account the superlative talents of Durnovo and his enemy Witte, both of them advocates of a strong monarchical power.

embarrassment its outcome caused his regime. As he pointed out, "It was precisely in those regions where the percentage of Bolshevik votes in November 1917 was lowest that we observe the greatest success of counterrevolutionary movements . . . Precisely in these regions did Kolchak and Denikin hold on for months and months." And again, "The results of the election to the Constituent Assembly in November 1917 provide the background for the spectacle of civil war as it develops in the course of the next two years." [42] The Soviet government would hold the heart of the country while its enemies would be constrained to operate on the periphery — an inestimable advantage for the one and a fateful handicap for the other. The Soviet government, though badly beaten in the election, had strength where it counted most and would be able to muster enough force "in decisive spots at the decisive moment" — the words are Lenin's — to overcome its enemies and wrest from their hands the leadership of the soft-bodied Russian peasantry.[43]

[42] "Vybory v Uchreditelnoe Sobranie i diktatura proletariata," *Sochineniia* (2nd ed.), XXIV, 643, 644.

[43] This line of thought is developed in *ibid.*, pp. 634–636, 638–644.

CHAPTER IV

THE QUESTION OF VALIDITY: HOW FREE WAS THE VOTE?

THE CORRELATION between the results of the election and the lines drawn in the civil war is sufficient evidence in itself that the vote in November of 1917 was an authentic expression of the will of the Russian people. In examining the validity of an election, it is necessary to weigh two factors: the degree of fraud and intimidation and the degree of public consciousness. Was the Russian citizen reasonably free to make a choice among the contending parties, and if so, did he have any real understanding of what he was doing when he made the choice? The validity of the returns will now be examined on the basis of these two criteria, and an attempt will be made to lessen the skepticism of those who doubt that a real election could be held under the Soviet regime or that the Russian voter could stand out from the herd in the exercise of his individual judgment.

First, then, how free was the vote? There is no end of complaint in the contemporary records about intimidation of the voting public, and no absence of "incidents" at the polls or in the course of the campaign. Responsibility for such offenses is usually attributed to the Bolsheviks as people with a penchant for violence and freedom to indulge it, now that they controlled the government and had disposal of the bayonets of the garrison troops, in addition to their own private apparatus of terrorism (the Red Guard and so on). The most effective and certainly the most ubiquitous propagandists of the Bolshevik cause were the soldiers from the front and the sailors from the Baltic Fleet, men whose methods of agitation tended to be simple and direct. Trained in the violence of war, they easily resorted to that technique in dealing with the opposition; fervently desiring an end of war, they were furious at those who would not accept Lenin's formula for immediate peace.[1] Within the barracks it was often unhealthy for a soldier to betray a preference for a party other than the Bolshevik,[2] and outside the barracks the soldiers sought to intimidate the civilian population by tearing down posters of rival parties, by destroying their lists,[3] and by threatening the lives and property of obdurate citizens.

Some instances may be cited. Saratov had always been a turbulent province — it was there that Stolypin had won his spurs as governor — and it sustained its reputation on this occasion. The socialist opposition felt the wrath of the soldiers as much or more than the bourgeoisie.[4] In Odessa, on the other hand, the Kadets bore the brunt of the soldiers' hostility.[5] In Kostroma

---

[1] As a soldier in Saratov put it, "Nothing matters except to end this damned war and get home" (quoted in the *Saratovskii Listok*, no. 241 [November 14, 1917]).

[2] *Russkiia Vedomosti*, no. 259 (November 26, 1917), where conditions in the Kozlov garrison are described in a letter; *Delo Naroda*, no. 214 (November 19, 1917), where a Menshevik protest against conditions in the XII Army is aired.

[3] This study is not concerned with the mechanics of voting. For the sake of clarity, however, it may be pointed out that there was no general ballot but rather a separate list of candidates for each party contesting the election in a given district (*okrug*). Each list bore a number, determined by the order of reception in the district in question. The voter was furnished with a list for each party, either by mail before the election or at the polling place upon demand. He chose the list of his preference and put it in an envelope, sealed the envelope and deposited it in the urn. The unwanted lists he discarded. The voter could choose only as between parties; once settled on a list, he had to take it as it was, not being able either to change the order of candidates or strike out a name. In Saratov some SR voters scratched Kerenski and had their ballots invalidated as a result (*Saratovskii Vestnik*, no. 245, November 15, 1917; *Saratovskii Listok*, no. 242, November 16, 1917). The "Belgian" or d'Hondt system of proportional representation was followed. See in general *Sputnik izbiratelia v Uchreditelnoe Sobranie* (Petrograd, 1917); simple explanations of voting system in *Russkoe Slovo*, no. 257 (November 24, 1917); *Delo Naroda*, no. 207 (November 12, 1917); more detailed explanation in O. A. Volkenstein, *Proportsionalnye vybory v Uchreditelnoe Sobranie* (Petrograd, 1917).

[4] *Saratovskii Listok*, no. 239 (November 11, 1917); *Saratovskii Vestnik*, no. 244 (November 14, 1917); report from Saratov in *Fakel*, no. 1 (November 25, 1917); report of Ina Rakitnikova in *Delo Naroda*, no. 232 (December 14, 1917).

[5] *Utro Rossii*, no. 261 (November 14, 1917).

province scenes reminiscent of tsarist times took place: soldiers arrived in the villages and behaved in challenging fashion, going everywhere armed and resorting freely to threats.[6] A priest in Riazañ province stated that when peasants' wives came to him to ask how to vote, they cast fearful glances over their shoulders, for Bolshevik soldiers had made the rounds of the village, declaring that everyone not voting their way would be known and would have his livestock, his grain, and his hut destroyed or taken away.[7] In Kozlov *uezd* of Tambov province agitators from the front sometimes threatened to kill their opponents.[8] For soldiers' wives they had a special argument: "If you don't vote for No. 7, just wait till your mate gets home — he'll beat the hell out of you!" [9]

But the offenses were not all on one side. The Bolsheviks had their grievances, too. It must be remembered that they did not control the electoral machinery, which carried over from the Provisional Government; and if they had the support of the highly articulate military element,[10] they also had the bitter opposition of other articulate elements, notably the schoolteachers, clergy, and kulaks. Though the schoolteacher was almost invariably an SR and the priest an adherent of the Kadet party or some other grouping still further to the right, they joined hands at times to

[6] Report on eve of the IV Congress, PSR, *Delo Naroda*, no. 220 (November 30, 1917).

[7] Alexander Drozdov, "Po Rossii: Slepaia Rossiia (Provintsialnyia vpechatleniia)," *Nash Vek*, no. 21 (December 23, 1917).

[8] *Russkiia Vedomosti*, no. 259 (November 26, 1917).

[9] See the informative correspondence from Kozlov, signed A. S., in *Delo Naroda*, no. 242 (December 28, 1917). The author is doubtlessly A[nastasia] S[lëtova], the wife of Chernov and in her own right one of the key figures in the SR organization in the black-earth zone, the center of party strength. She was one of the deputies elected from Tambov province. No. 7 was the Bolshevik list in that province.

[10] Not all the soldier propagandists, of course, agitated in favor of Bolshevism. Many worked for the PSR (see *ibid.* and N. Arepev, "Derevnia i Uchreditelnoe Sobranie," *Delo Naroda*, no. 236 (December 19, 1917); the latter describes the campaign in a canton of Tver province). But the SR soldiers seem to have lacked the verve and belligerence of their Bolshevik rivals. As for the Baltic sailors, they had a fanaticism all their own and were never anything except Bolshevik in sentiment.

combat the common enemy: thus in the village of Kandaurovka in Samara province the schoolmistress Bolshakova, with the aid of the local priest, forced the peasants to vote SR by snatching Bolshevik lists from their hands and by threatening their arrest in case of resistance; [11] while in a rural precinct of Pskov province the peasants — here apparently made of sterner stuff — chased the teacher away for having practiced deception at the polls (he was the presiding officer) and beat up the priest for having influenced the women in favor of the class enemy.[12] Bolshevik accounts of the election would not be Bolshevik if evil were not ascribed to those traditional scapegoats, the kulaks; yet there is no reason to doubt that the better-to-do peasants tried to turn the village against the party that menaced their class with extinction, using for that purpose means of suasion which ranged from subtle suggestion [13] to crude acts of physical violence — if we can believe the Soviet sources, one of which charges that in Saratov province peasants daring to vote the Bolshevik ticket were not infrequently beaten by the kulaks.[14] The Bolsheviks also suffered in other ways. Their agitation was trammeled or banned outright in some places, as in Spassko-Kashminskaia canton, Morshansk *uezd*, Tambov province, where the SR-dominated local administration justified its action on the grounds that the Bolsheviks were really German spies.[15] Another grievance was that something might happen to the party lists — their distribution might be delayed, or they might arrive in insufficient quantity, or they might never

[11] *Pravda*, no. 213 (December 13, 1917).

[12] *Derevenskaia Bednota*, no. 32 (November 18, 1917). The reverend father tore himself loose and ran away howling.

[13] See report from Pskov province, *ibid.*, no. 38 (November 25, 1917).

[14] V. P. Antonov-Saratovski, *Pod stiagom proletarskoi borby: Otryvki iz vospominanii o rabote v Saratove za vremia s 1915g. do 1918g.*, Vol. I (Moscow-Leningrad, 1925), p. 237. Sometimes the people were simply warned that the Bolsheviks were robbers and plunderers, and that those who followed them would be flogged with *nagaikas* (a Cossack's whip), as in 1905 — a reference to events still green in the memory of the Saratov peasantry.

[15] Report of G. Generalov, *Pravda*, no. 194 (November 19, 1917).

reach the voters at all.[16] The general effect in such cases was to leave the SR's a clear field for the election.

Hostilities were not confined to the Bolshevik and SR parties, and it is by no means necessary to rely solely on Bolshevik testimony for evidence of wrongdoing on the part of the opposition, particularly the SR opposition, composed as it was of so many self-righteous people. From the distant north comes a plaint from a peasant who adhered to the Kadet party, to the effect that the Ust-Sysolsk electoral commission of Vologda province, whose official duty it had been to explain all party programs to the voters, actually had carried out its mission in such a one-sided manner as to rig the election in favor of the PSR. In this work of perversion, the propagandists dispatched to the villages in the guise of official instructors had the full coöperation of the local authorities, who refused to give out the programs of other parties and demanded support for their own.[17] Down in the Ukraine, in fertile Poltava province, the Selianska Spilka or "Village Union," a powerful organization completely dominated by the Ukrainian Socialist Revolutionaries, had been guilty of excesses in its campaign against the Landowners' or Farmers' party, the lists of which were suppressed and its representatives excluded from the local electoral commissions.[18] Sometimes matters were carried to the point of terrorism, for we read that in Sokiriantsy village the

[16] *Izvestiia Moskovskago Soveta*, no. 232 (December 16, 1917), which cites instances of delay until the very day of the election in rural districts of Pskov, Vologda, Viatka, and Vitebsk provinces; *Pravda*, no. 200 (November 26, 1917), no. 208 (December 7, 1917). For abuses committed at the expense of the Bolsheviks, see in general *Pravda*, no. 202 (November 30, 1917), no. 3 (January 5, 1918); N. Rubinstein, *Bolsheviki i Uchreditelnoe Sobranie* (n.p., 1938), pp. 51–52; AOR, *Vserossiiskoe Uchreditelnoe Sobranie*, pp. 209–210, n. 12.

[17] Letter of Ilarion Sharapov, *Severnoe Ekho*, no. 99 (December 20, 1917). This newspaper was published in Vologda and was Kadet in tone if not in affiliation.

[18] Generally referred to as *zemlevladeltsy* (landowners), the adherents of this movement in the Ukraine are more frequently termed *khleboroby*, the proper translation of which is "farmers." There were more real farmers, of course, in the Ukraine than in Great Russia (farmers, that is, in the sense of peasant proprietors).

priest had suffered indignities — he was locked in jail, struck on the nose, and threatened with being torn to pieces — all because he belonged to the Landowners' party.[19] There were instances when peasants appeared before the authorities and begged on bended knees for some paper certifying that they were not members of the hated party; otherwise, they declared, their lives would be in danger.[20] Thus the use of nefarious tactics was by no means restricted to the Bolshevik party.

And yet side by side with this record of intimidation and violence another record could be compiled, bearing witness to the fact that in many places the voting passed off smoothly and without serious infractions of the electoral code. Let us take the case of the big cities. In Petrograd the outstanding feature of the election was its humdrum character. There was no especial enthusiasm, and no marked excesses, aside from the Red Guard's descent on the offices of the *Rech* the night of November 12.[21] A total absence of violence was noted in certain sections of the city — Moskovski, Liteinyi, Spasski, Vasilevski — and if local sentiment made it impossible for the Kadets to campaign on the Vyborg side,[22] they were very active in the Kazanski district; while along the Kriukov Canal even monarchist agitation could be observed.[23] The central organ of the PSR, the *Delo Naroda*, is hard put to find something wrong with the election; thus it ascribes a privileged position in the pre-electoral campaign to the Bolsheviks because of their monopoly of motor transport, only to contradict itself in the very same issue by speaking of automobiles in the service of the Kadets.[24] Even more impressive is the record in Moscow, where the fairness of the election is attested by all sources without exception. The Menshevik organ conceded that

---

[19] A reading of the record leads one to the conclusion that priests must have had a hard time of it during this election.

[20] D., "Vybory v Poltavskoi gubernii," *Nash Vek*, no. 18 (December 20, 1917).

[21] The *Rech* was the central organ of the Kadet party.

[22] A proletarian center and stronghold of Bolshevism.

[23] *Delo Naroda*, nos. 208, 209 (November 13, 14, 1917).

[24] See "Na ulitse," in *ibid.*, no. 208.

no ground existed for contesting the election,[25] and even the conservative *Russkoe Slovo*, while duly noting certain minor disorders at the polls, was constrained to admit that the Kadets enjoyed full civic rights and were able to contend on virtually even terms with the dominant party.[26] This is a remarkable circumstance in view of the hard fighting that had attended the October Revolution in Moscow and the blood-letting so recently past. Not only from the metropolitan centers but also from the country at large come reports of a quiet and orderly election. From Kostroma in the north to the Crimea in the south, from the Roumanian Front in the west to Vladivostok on the Pacific — from Tver, Tula, Minsk, Kiev, Podolia, Odessa, Ekaterinoslav province, Tambov, Penza, Samara, Simbirsk, Kazañ, Perm, Kars, Erivan, Tomsk, Irkutsk, and Blagoveshchensk — come accounts of normal conditions of voting.[27]

How, then, are we to reconcile this welter of conflicting evidence? A careful consideration of all the factors involved leads inevitably to the conclusion that the normal aspects of the election far outweigh the irregularities, numerous though these may be. Overshadowing everything else is the circumstance that the Bolsheviks had the power and lost the election. The results speak for themselves. There is not the slightest evidence on the government's part of a master plan to subvert the election or falsify the returns. The indubitable freedom of voting in the large cities shows that Lenin's regime did not intend to overawe the voters where it had the physical means of doing so, and elsewhere it was too newly established and administratively too weak to have done this even had it desired. True, there was a huge Bolshevik

---

[25] *Klich*, no. 1 (November 23, 1917).

[26] No. 255 (November 21, 1917). See also the account in *Russkiia Vedomosti*, no. 255 (November 21, 1917), and the report telephoned to Petrograd in *Delo Naroda*, no. 215 (November 21, 1917).

[27] *Delo Naroda*, nos. 209, 211, 212, 214, 218 (November 14, 16, 17, 19, 24, 1917); Sviatitski in *ibid.*, no. 227 (December 8, 1917); *Russkoe Slovo*, nos. 255, 257 (November 21, 24, 1917); *Volia Narodnaia*, no. 1 (November 28, 1917); *Izvestiia Vserossiiskoi po delam o vyborakh v Uchreditelnoe Sobranie Komissii*, no. 21 (November 22, 1917), p. 15, and no. 22 (November 29, 1917), p. 32.

vote both in Petrograd and in Moscow, but in neither city did it reach quite 50 per cent of the total, and few would contend that the percentages attained were excessive as a measure of strength of this proletarian party in the chief proletarian centers of the empire.

Furthermore, the record of fraud and violence on close inspection is not impressive. Of actual breakdowns in the conduct of the election (aside from postponements due to technical difficulties) we hear almost nothing — the only clear-cut instance of soldiers' interference breaking up the election is in Salopinski canton of Kaluga province — an area so small as not to merit consideration.[28] There were very few slayings, considering the extent of the country and the size of the population. The chairman of the Krasnikovo electoral commission in Orël province was killed by soldiers when he tried to restrain their illegal actions; [29] another such official, in this case a priest, was slain in Pskov province; [30] the Menshevik mayor of Bakhmut lost his life under circumstances that were not explained in the press [31] — and that was about all. As many fatalities have occurred at election time in the single state of Kentucky.

For the most part attempts at intimidation seem to have stopped at oral threats; they were spontaneous and sporadic, and without marked effect on the results. In turbulent Saratov province the Bolsheviks lost to the SR's by a ratio better than 2:1; [32] the fact that they did relatively well in this black-earth district was due not merely to the strong-armed tactics of the Saratov garrison, but also to the presence of a first-class industrial center, the city of Tsaritsyn, now known as Stalingrad. Though Kozlov *uezd*

---

[28] *Delo Naroda*, no. 212 (November 17, 1917). In addition, the SR organ accused the Bolsheviks of disrupting the election in Rzhëv *uezd* of Tver province (*ibid.*, no. 218, November 24, 1917), but it is not clear what happened in that locality.

[29] *Russkiia Vedomosti*, no. 253 (November 18, 1917); *Sovremennost*, no. 1 (November 23, 1917); *Utro Rossii*, no. 265 (November 18, 1917).

[30] *Sovremennost*, no. 1 (November 23, 1917).

[31] *Fakel*, no. 1 (November 25, 1917).

[32] See Chapter II, note 4.

of Tambov province, as we have seen, counted a large number of soldier propagandists who threatened to deal out death to their opponents, and no less than fifty of the redoubtable Baltic sailors who preached the same fiery message of Bolshevism, the degree of actual violence was small, much smaller than would have been necessary to save the government party from a decisive beating.[33] According to another source, the reaction of the peasantry here varied in the face of such provocation, the entire population in some villages bowing to force and casting only Bolshevik ballots, whereas in others like Tarbeev the inhabitants beat the Bolshevik bullies and threw them out of the polling place.[34] Both sources agree that in some places the Bolsheviks beat their foes, and in others were beaten by them. Here in a *uezd* out in the sticks we probably have in microcosm a true picture of what was going on all over Russia, the violence and pressure on one side being offset by similar tactics on the other, the result being a balanced election. There probably is a residue of illegality, however, on the side of the Bolsheviks, but not a large enough one to influence materially the outcome.

Nor was that outcome affected to any appreciable extent by the more subtle means of swinging an election such as are practiced in Western lands — illegal voting, stuffing the ballot box, falsification of returns, and so on. Undoubtedly some double-voting took place, particularly in the case of garrison troops,[35] and here and there protests were voiced at the theft or suppression of ballots — as by the Mensheviks at Motovilikha in the Urals,[36]

---

[33] Letter of A[nastasia] S[lëtova], *Delo Naroda*, no. 242 (December 28, 1917).

[34] *Russkiia Vedomosti*, no. 259 (November 26, 1917).

[35] See the warning proclamation of Mayor Shreider of Petrograd in *Vestnik gorodskogo samoupravleniia* (*Vedomosti Petrogradskago Gradonachalstva*), no. 118(203) (November 12, 1917). Soldiers were not infrequently provided with more than one qualifying certificate because of confusion about their home and military addresses. See also "Vybornyia nedorazumeniia," *Russkoe Slovo*, no. 255 (November 21, 1917).

[36] *Klich*, no. 1 (November 23, 1917). Here there was a big nest of Bolsheviks (Motovilikha is an industrial suburb of Perm).

or by the rightists in a village of Kostroma province [37] — but these were strictly isolated incidents and, all told, would add up to relatively little. Only in the case of Smolensk was a district electoral commission so thoroughly dissatisfied with conditions under which voting took place as to pose the question of a reëlection.[38]

The best evidence of the basic soundness of the returns is afforded by the controversy that arose in the capital between the Council of People's Commissars and the All-Russian Electoral Commission. Apparently the Bolsheviks, or at least some of their leaders, expected to come out ahead with the help of the Left SR's [39] until they saw the handwriting on the wall as returns from the black-earth zone began pouring in during the second week of the balloting. They realized then that most of the SR deputies would adhere to the centrist or right-wing factions of that huge but disintegrating party; [40] they were seized with alarm and, shrilly accusing the Commission of falsification and other abuses, decreed its arrest on November 23, only to release it a few days later without having substantiated the charges.[41] Thereafter a commission of surveillance was set up under Uritski and the

[37] *Russkoe Slovo*, no. 257 (November 24, 1917).

[38] *Delo Naroda*, no. 213 (November 18, 1917).

[39] See statement of Lunacharski, quoted in *ibid.*, no. 209 (November 14, 1917).

[40] The Bolsheviks never made any distinction between the numerically preponderant center under Chernov and the influential right wing, friendly to Kerenski; both were lumped together as "right SR's."

[41] It is interesting to note that on the preceding day a report had been received from Oboian *uezd*, Kursk province, crediting the SR's with 70,000 votes and the Bolsheviks with only 3,000 (*ibid.*, no. 216, November 22, 1917). This was the first decisive indication of how the vote would go in the populous black-earth region. The early returns were nearly all from towns and the Bolsheviks had been ahead. Then the rural returns began to accumulate and by November 26 the SR's were in the lead. See country-wide totals in the *Russkoe Slovo*, no. 259 and *passim*.

It may be added that the charges against the Commission have never been substantiated. For refutation of charges see *Delo Naroda*, nos. 228, 229 (December 9, 10, 1917). Full account of the affair may be found in *Izvestiia Vserossiiskoi po delam o vyborakh v Uchreditelnoe Sobranie Komissii*, no. 22 (November 29, 1917), pp. 1–28.

bickering continued, the assembling of returns now being more difficult than ever, but since the returns received continued to be as unfavorable to the Bolsheviks as before, the conclusion is inescapable that neither the All-Russian Commission nor the Soviet authorities were guilty of falsification.

On the basis of all the available evidence, therefore, it is safe to say that the first criterion of a valid election has been met in this instance: although a good many voters were subjected to intimidation in one form or another, and what went into the urns was not always what came out, the vast majority of the electorate freely exercised the right of suffrage and could be sure that its ballots would be counted as cast. It was far from being a model election, but it certainly was not a farce.

CHAPTER V

THE QUESTION OF VALIDITY: DID THE PEOPLE
KNOW WHAT THEY WERE DOING?

WE ARE NOW READY for the second criterion — the consciousness
of the voting public. Here we are in deep water from the outset,
owing to the intangible character of some of the factors involved,
the prejudice exhibited on every hand, the absence of real illumination amid an ocean of verbiage, and — worst of all — the
silence of the records on certain crucial matters. Loquaciousness
would hardly be what it is if it did not flow where it is not needed
and were not shut off where it would be welcome.

The view has been expressed that the results of the election to
the All-Russian Constituent Assembly were somehow not representative of the Russian people, that the Russian peasant was
innately a conservative creature who would have supported the
Church and the Tsar, or at the very least the Kadets, had his mind
not been befuddled by the fumes of revolutionary propaganda.
The essence of the Constitutional Democratic program — the
combination of a belief in universal suffrage with defense of the
institution of private property — was predicated upon this as-
sumption. And the Union of Monarchists proclaimed soon after
the results became known that it would never recognize the
authority of a body chosen under conditions of fraud and violence, in the absence of which a monarchist majority would have
been assured.[1] At the other end of the political spectrum, and
equally scornful of the results, are the Bolsheviks, one of whose
leaders has asserted that a delay of even a month in holding the
election would have permitted his party, through further intensive

[1] See comment of N. S. Rusanov, "Chernaia sotnia i krasnaia," *Delo
Naroda*, no. 221 (December 1, 1917); "Chernaia sotnia shevelitsia," *Izvestiia
Tsentralnago Ispolnitelnago Komiteta i petrogradskago soveta*, no. 240
(November 30, 1917), p. 4.

cultivation of the peasantry, to secure control of the Assembly.[2] Sweeping assertions of this sort, insofar as they do not rest upon wishful thinking, are based upon two widely observed phenomena in 1917: first, a startling fluctuation of party strength in the towns and, second, the success enjoyed by divergent groups in propagandizing the peasants. In the first case the inference is that the parties had no following in the true sense of the word, and in the second, that the country population resembled a flock of sheep which could be herded in any direction. Let us now examine critically each of these phenomena, after which we may be able to determine whether or not the detractors of the election are justified in their contentions.

The shifting of votes from one political camp to another attained truly formidable proportions and occurred in an amazingly short interval of time. It is to be seen in a comparison of the results in local elections with those of the general election to the Constituent Assembly and is restricted to the towns, for it is impossible to measure sentiment in the village before the November balloting. The outstanding example is the city of Moscow, where the SR's swept the field in the June vote for the central municipal council, only to sustain a catastrophic defeat in the September election to municipal district councils, followed by the final rout in November (see accompanying tabulation).[3]

[2] Antonov, *Pod stiagom proletarskoi borby*, I, 238. See also Uritski's report to the Petrograd Bolshevik Committee in L. Trotski, *Sochineniia* (Moscow, n.d.), III, Part II, 364, 367. Uritski contended that the new regime had not had enough time to get its program across to the population in more remote parts of the country. But for this, it would have secured "at least a majority."

[3] Table of comparison in *Russkiia Vedomosti*, no. 257 (November 24, 1917). As only round figures are given, it is not reproduced here. The figures given here are from the following sources: June election, *Russkoe Slovo*, no. 149 (July 2, 1917); September election, *ibid.*, no. 222 (September 29, 1917); November election, *Russkiia Vedomosti*, no. 257 (November 24, 1917).

Party	June	September	November
SR	374,885	54,374	62,260
Bolshevik	75,409	198,320	366,148
Kadet	108,781	101,106	263,859
Menshevik	76,407	15,887	21,597
Others	11,086	16,160	50,899
Total vote	646,568	385,847	764,763

Expressed in terms of percentage, the vote for the major parties was as follows:

Party	June	September	November
SR	58	14	8
Bolshevik	12	51	48
Kadet	17	26	35
Menshevik	12	4	3

In Petrograd the same tendency is apparent, though not to the same degree: [4]

Party	August	November
SR	205,666	152,230
Bolshevik	183,694	424,027
Kadet	114,485	246,506
Menshevik	23,552	29,167
Others	21,982	90,403
Total vote ..	549,379	942,333

What kind of an electorate was it that could give a party an absolute majority in June and then slash its vote to 14 per cent in September and 8 per cent in November? Is it possible even to speak of political consciousness in the face of such a demonstra-

[4] Figures for August election to city council from *Delo Naroda*, no. 136 (August 25, 1917); November figures from *ibid.*, nos. 211, 212 (November 16, 17, 1917). In May the district or ward councils had been filled (the order was the reverse of that in Moscow). Because of bloc voting and diffusion of returns, however, it is not possible to give a clear picture of party strength in the May election.

tion of political volatility? In Saratov it had been only less catastrophic than in Moscow: the moderate socialists had seen their following shrink from 37,564 in July to 12,798 in November, a loss of a good two-thirds; more than 10,000 voters had deserted to the "bourgeois" camp, and within the socialist fold itself, nearly 15,000 had switched their allegiance to Bolshevism.[5] As the Saratov editor observed, these floaters were not really adherents of socialism or, indeed, of anything else and hence could not be ascribed to the party of their momentary choice; only the Popular Socialists had possessed a stable following from summer to fall, and that a very small one. Where no stability of partisan sympathies obtained, there could be no talk of political consciousness.[6]

And yet what had happened was typical of any revolution: the decomposition of the center and the building up of the extremes as the revolution deepened. From the swamp of political repression the Russian citizen had emerged onto the stream of political freedom, and it was necessary for him to get his bearings, identifying himself with one or the other of the unfamiliar objects suddenly appearing on the surface. As the stream was flowing so swiftly, it is not surprising that he floundered about, grasping first at one support and then at another. The early elections had taken place on a local scale and during the honeymoon stage of the revolution. What more splendid receptacle could have been provided for the votes of bewildered citizens, their hearts filled with enthusiasm and their heads with nebulous ideas, than the Socialist Revolutionary party? But the revolution wore on and the honeymoon spirit wore off; the passions loosed by Kornilov's August rebellion and Lenin's October Revolution tore the mask of romanticism from the face of the class struggle, and the urban masses lurched to the right or the left, parting the center and clearing the field for civil war. The ranks of Bolshevism swelled and likewise those

[5] The comparison here requires no adjustment, as the total vote is almost identical (60,025 in the July municipal election and 60,182 in November).

[6] *Saratovskii Vestnik*, no. 248 (November 18, 1917).

of Constitutional Democracy, establishing for the first time a kind of political equilibrium among parties that rested on a solid contingent of voters who would not desert at the next turn of the revolutionary wheel. It is true that Bolshevism numbered among its adherents many who went with the victor of the hour — the bandwagon vote, in other words — and that the Kadets sheltered elements of the right — perhaps very substantial elements — but each party had an irreducible core of strength which no doubt accounted for most of its following. Thus it was not the election to the Constituent Assembly but rather the earlier local elections which had registered an ephemeral sentiment; by November the lines had hardened, and the voters knew much better what they were doing than in preceding tests of sentiment.[7]

But what of the village? The able editor at Saratov had wrung his hands at the mere thought of it, exclaiming that if the electorate of a city called the "Athens of the Volga" could put on such an exhibition of political irresponsibility, then what must be the situation out in the country, amid the dark, dumb mass of the peasantry? The rustics, as we know, had favored the SR ticket. Was this merely an evidence of the customary lag of the village behind the town, or did it have some independent meaning? Sources of varied political inclination attest to the ease with which the peasant was influenced in 1917. To the reader it almost seems that whoever approached him last received his vote. The testimony is unanimous that soldiers swayed the mass at will and exerted a profound influence on the outcome of the election. Thus in the almost exclusively agrarian province of Chernigov the Bolshevik party, with no organization at all in most of the *uezds* and only a feeble one in others, nevertheless gained authority in

---

[7] The election figures for Moscow show that by fall the Bolshevik following had become stabilized. Not only did the October Revolution fail to increase the relative strength of the party — it could not even avert the loss of the absolute majority secured in September, the vote falling from 51 to 48 per cent. Although the opposition seized on this circumstance, it was of little significance in view of the much larger turnout at the polls (virtually a 100 per cent increase over September). It does minimize, however, the effect of the bandwagon vote.

the eyes of the people and received more than a quarter of a
million votes in November as a tribute to the zeal of soldiers
returning from the front.[8] The same phenomenon is observed in
widely separated parts of the country.[9] These men from the front
were as ubiquitous in the rear as their actions were energetic; not
even central Siberia was spared their visitations.[10] A beautiful
example of their influence is reported from Viazma: cantons near
the railroad line went for the Bolsheviks and those further away
for the SR's, simply because soldiers had worked the villages near
the stations but had not penetrated into the interior.[11] Sometimes, as in the Moscow industrial region, workers would take the
place of soldiers, going by droves into the backwoods with the
message of Bolshevism and presenting their party with an unex-
pected victory in unlikely places.[12] Only the shortage of propagandists circumscribed the scope of the victory, so fruitful were
the results of agitation, for all that was needed was to talk to the
simple folk in order to win them over.[13] The mood of the peasantry
could easily be changed, if we are to judge from what happened
in several cantons of Tver province, where a single agitator dis-
pelled the animosity to Bolshevism and won the populace over to
his cause.[14] At times the peasants betrayed their past by wanting

[8] V. K. Shcherbakov, *Zhovtneva revoliutsiia i roki gromadianskoï borotbi
na Chernigivshchini* (Chernigov, 1927), pp. 33–34 (written in Ukrainian).

[9] *Novaia Zhizn*, no. 201 (December 14, 1917), report from Minsk; *Delo
Naroda*, no. 220 (November 30, 1917), report from Kostroma; *ibid.*, no.
231 (December 13, 1917), report from Moscow province; *Pravda*, no. 194
(November 19, 1917), report from Kaluga; see *Russkoe Slovo*, no. 255
(November 21, 1917), for general comment.

[10] *Utro Rossii*, no. 279 (December 6, 1917); *Izvestiia Vserossiiskoi po
delam o vyborakh v Uchreditelnoe Sobranie Komissii*, no. 21 (November
22, 1917), p. 15, citing reports of pressure exerted by soldiers in the
Krasnoiarsk district.

[11] *Russkiia Vedomosti*, no. 258 (November 25, 1917).

[12] N. Meshcheriakov in *Izvestiia Moskovskago Soveta*, no. 217 (November 29, 1917).

[13] *Moskovskaia provintsiia v semnadtsatom godu*, ed. E. Popova (Moscow-Leningrad, 1927), pp. 154–155.

[14] "Vesti iz provintsii," *Derevenskaia Bednota*, no. 38 (November 25,
1917). Yet side by side with this must be set evidence of a contradictory
nature from still another canton in the same province: here a public

to be told how to vote,[15] and the inhabitants of one village, deciding that they had made a mistake, upbraided the authorities for having failed to send instructions: "Why weren't we, dark and ignorant people, told for whom to vote?" [16]

Is there no evidence whatever of a will of its own on the part of the Russian peasantry? And what if it were subjected simultaneously to opposing stimuli — how then would it react? Unfortunately, we have no real illumination of the temper of the village as it approached the urns, or of how it cast its vote. Scraps of information may painfully be put together, but the countless villages of Russia are the great dark province of the election. In the case of Kozlov *uezd* of Tambov province, however, conditions have been analyzed by a prominent political figure who was honest and intelligent; returns are available which are adequate if not complete; and location is such as to make it a typical constituency in the black-earth zone, where most of the Russian people have lived since the close of the seventeenth century. To afford a graphic illustration of the contrast between town and country, the figures for the *uezd* center, the town of Kozlov, are given alongside those of the *uezd* itself, exclusive of the town: [17]

---

meeting (*skhod*) had been called at the insistence of a Smolny agitator, and he was listened to, but the literature he passed out was torn up and the canton gave the SR's 12,000 votes to 1,400 for the Bolsheviks. Perhaps the explanation of his failure lies in the fact that in this locality soldiers returning from the front generally recommended the SR list (N. Arepev, "Derevnia i Uchreditelnoe Sobranie," *Delo Naroda*, no. 236, December 19, 1917).

[15] Al. Altaev, "Kak prokhodiat vybory v Uchreditelnoe Sobranie v derevne," *Derevenskaia Bednota*, no. 32 (November 18, 1917).

[16] Letter from Podoskliaia village, Nizhne-Spassk canton, Tambov *uezd*, to the *Tambovskii Zemskii Vestnik*, quoted in *Russkoe Slovo*, no. 247 (November 10, 1917). They had voted for the Coöperatives' list and now favored the SR's. Something is wrong, for it is stated that the balloting occurred on October 22, and November 12 (25) was the first day of voting. The author knows of no instance of voting before that date, albeit of plenty after it. Maybe the village jumped the gun.

[17] Town figures, *Russkoe Slovo*, no. 252 (November 17, 1917); *uezd* figures, *ibid.*, no. 256 (November 23, 1917).

	Civilian	Town Garrison	Total	Uezd
Registered	19,608	8,046	27,654	?
Voted	9,467	4,045	13,512	137,901
SR	?	?	1,642	96,033
Bolshevik	908	3,006	3,914	35,224
Kadet	?	?	5,107	2,997
Menshevik	?	?	1,902	1,856
Popular Socialist	?	?		366
Landowner	?	?	947	1,288
Mohammedan	?	?		137? [18]

Here on a scale smaller and therefore more revealing than for the provinces given before, the basic structure of the election is laid bare. The Kadets carried the town, but were swamped in the garrison and buried in the village. The Bolsheviks had the support of the peasants in uniform but not of those who were rooted in the soil. Nevertheless, this party of the proletariat had achieved a considerable following in a purely non-proletarian area, faring much better in the villages than in the town proper. How had these results been brought about? Certainly not by force and repression, the local aspects of which have already been considered. It is not necessary to conjecture in this instance — we know what happened. The parties had carried on a campaign that was not only free but rigorous. With the aid of secondary school students, who were middle class in background and nationalist in sentiment, the Kadets had made a strong bid for votes in the town, getting their campaign under way long before the twelfth of November. Their placards could be seen everywhere. But out in the country they made no headway whatever; there the SR's and the Bolsheviks held the field and no other party had even so much as a look-in. The fierce and prolonged agitation of the Bolshevik soldiers and sailors was not without its effect — the SR leader tells us that the people hearkened to their simple message, "he

[18] Difference between announced total vote and sum of vote by parties. May represent an error or may be vote cast for Moslem list, which is omitted from tabulation.

who is for peace, let him vote for us" — but on the whole they fought in vain against the intrenched position of the PSR with its manifold roots in the Tambov countryside,[19] its old and tested ties with the peasantry, and its corps of veteran workers. The SR's countered the soldiers' propaganda by bringing in their own men from the front, and party supporters in the trenches wrote home, advising their relatives to choose the SR list. In this manner the all-powerful influence of the front was divided and arrayed against itself. The election on the whole passed off normally: no one was killed and of the few who were beaten, some were on one side and some on the other.[20]

What happened, then, is reasonably clear. In this sleepy provincial town of Kozlov, a trading center with little industry and no proletariat to speak of, the Kadets had staged a determined effort under the very nose of the garrison and had achieved a large plurality. As in Petrograd and Moscow, the middle class had given them its vote. But that was all. Their activity did not extend beyond the town for the very simple reason there was no social element they could appeal to except the landowners. They had nothing to say to the peasants that the peasants wanted to hear. The Russian village was invincibly determined to have the land of the nobility and pay nothing for it, and the stand of the Kadets for compensation, however justified it may have been legally or morally, had no other effect than to erect an insuperable barrier to party work in the village.[21] It did no good to argue the rights of private property — there was no class of peasant

[19] Here the foundations of the party had been laid by V. M. Chernov, his wife, A. N. Slëtova, his brother-in-law, Stephen Slëtov, and their associates in the last decade of the preceding century. See Chernov, *Zapiski sotsialista-revoliutsionera*, Book I (Berlin, Petersburg and Moscow, 1922), pp. 249*ff*.

[20] Account of A[nastasia] S[lëtova] in *Delo Naroda*, no. 242 (December 28, 1917).

[21] One illustration of this: the peasants in Subochinskaia canton, Petrograd province, shouted down a Kadet speaker who attempted to present his party's program. The Bolshevik agitator overcame his SR rivals; the Kadet was not even heard (*Derevenskaia Bednota*, no. 38, November 25, 1917).

proprietors, no farming element, to appreciate such arguments. The Kadets lost the village, not because of the revolution, but because of the heritage of the old regime. Nothing kept them from the village except the temper of the village itself.

If the SR's could easily outbid the Kadets for the peasants' favor, the Bolsheviks could go beyond the SR's. They could tax their rivals with delaying the land reform and they could promise an immediate end to war. Slëtova tells us that for the most part the Bolsheviks got their votes from the villages near town (*prigorodnyia sëla*) and from the women; [22] although she does not explain why this was so, we may readily conjecture that the villages near town were those most worked over by the garrison, and that the women wanted to get their men home from the front. So there were thousands and thousands of peasant votes for Lenin's party, but the mass still preferred the party which first had brought it the message of Land and Liberty and which it knew from old association.

That the peasantry was vitally interested in the election is attested by the extraordinarily high turnout at the polls. The degree of participation in the *uezd* as a whole stood at 86 per cent and in some cantons it exceeded 90 per cent — figures that cannot be matched in any free election in the West and that are scarcely surpassed in a dictator's plebescite. The mood of the village was solemn and exalted as it prepared to vote: though the villagers would not listen for a moment to the political advice of the priest, they were not ready to dispense with the services of his cult, and so the church bells were rung and a *Te Deum* celebrated, after which virtually the whole population thronged to the polling-place, it mattered not that the weather was miserable and the roads were out. The enthusiasm of the rural population stands in striking contrast to the apathy of the townspeople, less than half of whom

[22] She states that secrecy of the ballot was a farce in the village; everyone knew what everyone else was going to do. In addition to the women, the village youth appears to have furnished many recruits for Bolshevism; at least that was the impression of an eye-witness in Riazañ province (Drozdov, "Po Rossii: Slepaia Rossiia [Provintsialnyia vpechatleniia]," *Nash Vek*, no. 21, December 23, 1917).

took the trouble to vote; even the garrison, about whose activity we hear so much, made only a mediocre showing.

We may conclude from the evidence at hand that there was nothing fundamentally wrong with the election in Kozlov *uezd*. When burghers vote for property rights, soldiers and their wives for peace and demobilization, and peasants for land, what is there about the spectacle that is abnormal or unreal? True, comprehension of party programs was rudimentary and attachment to party names perfunctory, but in an elemental way the electorate knew what it was doing. The degree of consciousness was not high, but it is foolish to contend that none existed.

The question now arises of how typical Kozlov *uezd* was of Russia as a whole. The answer is that it affords a cross-section of the black-earth zone but not necessarily of other regions. The peasantry of the black earth offered sterner resistance to Bolshevism than the peasantry elsewhere, partly because the black-earth peasantry had only agrarian interests — in contrast to the mixed, half-peasant, half-proletarian class in the north — and partly because Social Revolutionism here on its home soil possessed a tradition and an organizational continuity with the past which made it a force to be reckoned with and enabled it to hold its lines much better than in other parts of the country where it resembled nothing so much as a mushroom, grown up overnight in the fetid atmosphere of 1917. The more sustained character of the party struggle here in the bread-basket of Russia imparts greater meaning to the election.

In other respects, however, Kozlov was representative of all sections of the country. In towns that were administrative or trading centers with little or no industrial life, it was not only frequently but usually the case for the Kadets to come out on top, and even the Mensheviks, who clung to the euphemistic title of United Social Democrats, not infrequently ran ahead of their Bolshevik rivals. It was not so much the weakness of these parties in the towns as the weakness of the towns in Russia which accounted for their poor showing. The garrisons, on the other hand, were nearly always strongholds of Bolshevism, and many a town would have registered an overwhelming defeat for that party had it not been saved by the soldiers' votes.[23] The same disproportion between the turnout in town and country that obtained in Kozlov *uezd* could be observed throughout the empire, though not always to the same degree. Nearly everywhere the town population [24] seemed dispirited and disillusioned in the Constituent Assembly, as though having a presentiment of what lay in store for that body after the October Revolution. The country people, however, still believed in the institution they thought would give them the land and attended the polls in great numbers, bringing with them the aged and the blind and voting with a lift of spirit unobserved elsewhere.[25] In the towns the portion of the electorate participating rarely rose as high as 70 per cent, usually did not exceed 50 per cent, and sometimes sank as low as 30 per cent, whereas in the country a participation of 60 to 80 per cent was the rule and even 90 per cent was not unknown. As a consequence, the normally vast preponderance of the village became vaster still.[26]

Thus the information pertaining to Kozlov *uezd* affords much insight into the character and conduct of the election, not only for that large portion of Russia comprising the black-earth zone but for other regions as well. There is one bit of information lacking, however, and it is of crucial importance. A dispatch in the

[23] Boris Nikolaevski, "Pervye itogi," *Klich*, no. 1 (November 23, 1917); *Fakel*, no. 1 (November 25, 1917); "Vybory v Uchreditelnoe Sobranie," *Russkiia Vedomosti*, no. 257 (November 24, 1917).

[24] The metropolitan centers are to some extent an exception. There the class struggle raged unabated and the attendance at the polls was better, reaching 65.4 per cent in Moscow and 71 per cent in Petrograd. It was the working class, however, that evinced the most interest; the middle class, and also the soldiers, lagged behind (*Delo Naroda*, nos. 209, 210, 212 [November 14, 15, 17, 1917]; *Volnost*, no. 25 [November 17, 1917]; *Russkoe Slovo*, no. 255 [November 21, 1917]).

[25] N. Arepev, "Derevnia i Uchreditelnoe Sobranie," *Delo Naroda*, no. 236 (December 19, 1917); *Russkoe Slovo*, no. 255 (November 21, 1917); *Novaia Zhizn*, no. 201 (December 14, 1917), report of Minsk correspondent; *Saratovskii Vestnik*, no. 252 (November 24, 1917), noting contrast in Khvalynsk *uezd*.

[26] *Russkiia Vedomosti*, no. 263 (December 1, 1917).

Russkiia Vedomosti, citing with approval the example of peasants who beat their tormenters and chased them from the polls, asserts that unfortunately such courage was not always forthcoming, and that in some villages the entire population bowed to threats and cast only Bolshevik ballots.[27] Are we to infer that the reverse was also true, and that in many villages hostile to Bolshevism only SR ballots were cast? If so, in how many? In Kozlov *uezd* 96,033 votes were recorded for the SR's and 35,224 for the Bolsheviks, a ratio of nearly 3:1. What does that mean? Does it mean that in the average village three of the inhabitants voted SR for every one that voted Bolshevik? Or does it mean that in four villages of approximately equal size, three voted solidly SR and one voted solidly Bolshevik? Could the Russian peasant exercise the right of suffrage as an individual or only as a member of a herd? In short, was this a genuine election, or only a measurement of the relative effect of divergent pressures playing upon an inert mass?

Unfortunately, such conjectures can not be dismissed as idle speculation. Besides the instance mentioned, there are other indications of herd voting. We are told that the rural population in the Taganrog area was all but unanimous in its support of the PSR.[28] Even more impressive is the testimony from Oboian *uezd* of Kursk province to the effect that entire cantons cast nothing but SR votes (in the *uezd* as a whole the Bolsheviks had only 3,000 and the Kadets 1,000 against 70,000 for the SR's).[29] The village commune in Great Russia functioned collectively in many ways; may it not have done so in regard to voting, especially when we consider that going to the polls appears to have been more a community than an individual affair?[30] Sometimes the peasants in a village declared they had made their choice and did

[27] No. 259 (November 26, 1917).

[28] *Klich,* no. 1 (November 23, 1917); *Delo Naroda,* no. 218 (November 24, 1917), which claims 95 per cent of the vote for the SR's.

[29] *Delo Naroda,* no. 216 (November 22, 1917).

[30] Arepev gives an interesting account of the electoral scene in a canton of Tver province (in *ibid.,* no. 236, December 19, 1917).

not wish to listen to any other party.[31] Yet the only two illuminating accounts we have of what went on in the village at the time of the election do not suggest that the vote was undivided. It was not the collective will of the village but the individual choice of the head of the household which decided the issue in the unnamed canton of Tver province; the other members of the household, as a rule, simply followed his example.[32] And the inference to be drawn from Slëtova's report on Kozlov *uezd* is that the votes of soldiers' wives, if nothing else, provided an element of dissent in SR villages.

But what of the returns themselves? What light do they shed on the subject of herd voting as a means of determining the level of political consciousness of the Russian village? It is precisely here that the investigator encounters a blank wall. There are no returns by villages. They are announced for towns, provinces, *uezds*, and in some cases for cantons, but even that does not help, for a canton consists of a number of villages and hence could give the appearance of a mixed vote even though certain villages might have gone all one way and others all the other way. Neither Sviatitski, nor Lenin, nor the Archives of the October Revolution give a single example of how the village voted, and one searches in vain through the maze of figures in the metropolitan press of 1917 for a clue to the solution of this question on which the whole character of the election hinges. In one single instance the central organ of the PSR printed the returns for a rural precinct in Simferopol *uezd*, Taurida province (the Crimea), not bothering to give the name of the precinct but being content to let the figures speak for themselves: [33]

SR	586
Bolshevik	1
Kadet	2
Mohammedan	53

[31] *Moskovskaia provintsiia v semnadtsatom godu* (ed. Popova), p. 155; Ina Rakitnikova, in *Delo Naroda*, no. 215 (November 21, 1917).

[32] Arepev. The authority of the family head is also emphasized in Ia. Levanidov, "Podgotovka k izbiratelnoi kampanii v derevne," *Delo Naroda*, no. 144 (September 2, 1917).

[33] *Ibid.*, no. 218 (November 24, 1917).

A total of three individualists [34] out of 642 voters makes the election look very bad indeed, until we remember that this must have been an extreme case, pulled out of the bag by the SR editors to point up their party's boast of being the "sovereign of the country's thoughts." Yet it was a stumbling block to any less pessimistic view of the election as long as there was nothing else to go on.

Finally, recourse was had to the provincial newspapers, rare and scattered though they be, and, after prolonged investigation, rescue came from the direction of Saratov. The excellent press of this "Athens of the Volga" printed a whole series of returns by villages for Saratov *uezd*, disclosing the nature of the rural vote in at least this one locality. A total of twenty-seven rural precincts form the basis of the study.[35] Three villages have been selected for presentation here, each being representative of a number of others and each being an authentic village — that is, not a settlement on the outskirts of Saratov city. The vote was divided as indicated in the tabulation on page 66.

It is quite obvious that the inhabitants of the first two villages moved as a mass without exercising their individual judgment, but it would be interesting to know why they moved in opposite directions. Perhaps in the one case there was some stimulus that did not prevail in the other, something that broke down the SR hegemony in Rybushka — if, as is likely, it once existed — but failed to shake it in Great Idolga.[36] We do not know. In any event a small minority stood out against the mass in both instances, daring to have a conviction of its own and daring to follow

[34] The 53 Tatars can not be considered as individualists since they were of a different race and religion — they belonged, in other words, to a different herd.

[35] A precinct does not necessarily coincide with a village. In many instances, however, this appears to have been the case — particularly in respect to larger villages (the usual type in Saratov province). The convenience of the voting public was the criterion, subject to administrative feasibility. See *Sputnik izbiratelia*, pp. 122–123.

[36] Both villages are given brief mention in *Rossiia: Polnoe geograficheskoe opisanie* (ed. Semenov), Vol. VI (1901), *Srednee i nizhnee Povolzhe i Zavolzhe*, pp. 482, 497.

	Great Idolga	Rybushka	Korsakovka
Registered	1,343	2,150	919
Voted	995*(74%)	1,638†(76%)	631 (69%)
List No:			
1 Kadet	8	0	2
2 SD Menshevik	0	0	1
3 Ukrainian and Tatar			
Bloc	0	25	0
4 Old Believer	0	0	86
5 Orthodox	3	12	3
6 Landowner	23	0	82
7 German	22	8	0
8 Popular Socialist ...	3	5	6
9 Faith and Order			
(rightist)	0	4	1
10 SD Bolshevik	64	1,516	127
11 Mordvin	0	0	0
12 SR	873	62	323

* Announced total. Total by parties one vote more.
† Announced total. Total by parties six votes less.

through. It is not large enough, however, to prevent the stock of the election from falling in the face of such returns. Then we turn to Korsakovka,[37] and the stock rises again. Here a real election was held. Here was no bovine stampede in one direction but rather a true diversity of opinion, reflected in a substantial vote for three other lists besides the leading one and in a sprinkling of votes over the rest of the field. Of the other twenty-four villages reported, ten were more or less like Great Idolga, three like Rybushka, and eleven like Korsakovka. In other words, fifteen villages gave an undue concentration [38] of votes to one party (eleven to the SR's and four to the Bolsheviks), twelve showed

[37] A village of Viazovka canton about 25 miles in a straight line north northwest of Saratov. Not mentioned in *ibid*. and can be located only on the most detailed maps in possession of the Hoover Library.

[38] This means two-thirds or more of the total vote. In order to deal with borderline cases, it is necessary to set an arbitrary standard. Only four precincts fall within the range 60–68 per cent.

a reasonable distribution among the parties,[39] and not a single one turned in a unanimous vote. That was the story for Saratov *uezd*, insofar as we have it.[40]

The returns presented, of course, are all from a district with a large urban center, the influence of which undoubtedly tended to radiate into the surrounding countryside, even though no extreme effect is noticeable in this instance. The villages cited were real ones. They were situated on fertile *chernozëm* and were highly productive, both in crops and in children, so that they were densely populated; since there was no lack of large estates to whet the greed — or revolutionary ardor — of the inhabitants, it was only natural that they should have favored either the SR's or the Bolsheviks.[41] Hence the returns are wholly admissible and may be used without hesitation.

Nevertheless, election figures for some locality remote from any suggestion of urban influence would be welcome, and it is possible to provide them in the case of three villages or precincts located in the same province but in a different *uezd*, the *uezd* of Khvalynsk, which occupies the northeastern corner of Saratov province and lies about halfway between Samara and Saratov, at a gratifying distance from both. Long a stronghold of the Old Believers because of its remote and secluded character, and having also its complement of sectarians, not excluding the orgiastic Khlysty and the dreadful Skoptsy, Khvalynsk *uezd* represents the backwoods of Russia in their most primitive form.[42] As a consequence, the returns in the accompanying table from Federovka village

---

[39] The leading party had less than half the vote in four of these, just over half in five others, and between 60–66 per cent in the remaining three.

[40] *Saratovskii Listok*, no. 247 (November 21, 1917), combined with *Saratovskii Vestnik*, no. 250 (November 21, 1917).

[41] Facts from *Rossiia: Polnoe geograficheskoe opisanie*, VI, 497–498.

[42] *Ibid.*, p. 460; N. Andreev, *Illiustrirovannyi putevoditel po Volge i eia pritokam Oke i Kame* (2nd ed.; Moscow, n.d.), pp. 240–241; A. Lepeshinskaia and B. Dobrynin, *Volga* (Moscow, 1911), pp. 176–181, where Khvalynsk is called the Old Believers' Palestine. The Old Believers rank as schismatics, not as sectarians. The Khlysty were flagellants; the Skoptsy sought purification through self-mutilation, especially of the sexual organs.

and from two other precincts in Federovka canton are highly to be prized.[43]

	Federovka Village	Vorobievski Precinct	Ershovski Precinct
Registered	1,290	not given	not given
Voted	847 *	not given	not given
List No:			
1 Kadet	46	0	4
2 SD Menshevik	0	0	0
3 Ukrainian and Tatar Bloc	0	0	0
4 Old Believer	92	8	456
5 Orthodox	16	3	13
6 Landowner	83	77	4
7 German	0	0	1
8 Popular Socialist ...	29	0	0
9 Faith and Order (rightist)	53	4	1
10 SD Bolshevik	58	1	46
11 Mordvin	0	0	0
12 SR	467	35	105

* Total by parties 844. Two votes were disallowed — one unaccounted for.

It is obvious that Ershovski and Vorobievski precincts are exceptional as far as voting preference is concerned; there were relatively few villages in the Russia of 1917 where the Old Believers would predominate (in the political sense), and fewer still where the hated landowners would come out on top. Only Federovka can qualify as representative in this sense, though even there the Bolshevik vote is abnormally low. But that is beside the point. The thing to note here is that in these backwoods there was no unanimity of sentiment nor even an approach to it. True, there is evidence of a mass reaction in the large vote compiled by a single favored list in each instance, but there were

[43] *Saratovskii Vestnik*, no. 251 (November 23, 1917). Federovka was a larger village (*selo*) located on a high bluff overlooking the Volga, into which it always seemed on the verge of sliding. Vorobievski and Ershovski possibly were lesser villages (*derevni*); they could not be located on map.

plenty of strays from the herd in all three villages. In Federovka a very large minority rejected the SR list and further affirmed its independence by splitting up its vote among seven parties. This was an unusually satisfactory dispersion of strength. And even in Ershovski precinct, where Old Ritualism retained something of its pristine vigor, twenty-three hold-outs preferred some other conservative list, and 151 votes were cast for the Revolution. Rural Russia, as reflected in these figures, does not look so bad as might have been expected.

In the entire province of Saratov, minus Kamyshin *uezd*, the SR's received 564,250 votes and the Bolsheviks 225,000.[44] Enough has been said to show the reader that, unfortunately, these totals were not amassed in any such healthy fashion as a 5:2 division in the average village, but rather in large part by a top-heavy vote for the Bolsheviks in many villages, overbalanced by an equally top-heavy vote for the SR's in a much greater number of villages. Yet it must be remembered, also, that to a considerable extent the totals were amassed in thoroughly legitimate fashion by the inclusion of returns from a large number of settlements like Korsakovka,[45] where there had been a real division of opinion and, consequently, a real election.

[44] See Chapter II, note 4. The other ten lists drew 165,309 votes.
[45] Here, incidentally, the ratio between the leading parties was 323:127 or almost exactly 5:2.

CHAPTER VI

CONCLUSION

As WE COME to our conclusion, then, the image before us in respect to the validity of this election is neither all black nor all white; it is rather a somber gray. The village vote is indubitably the Achilles' heel of the election. In the towns the vote was along class lines and there is every indication that it was a fairly conscious one, the only defect being an indifferent turnout at the polls. But in the villages an inferior political consciousness permitted the populace to be swayed now one way and now the other, depending upon the intensity and the persistence of the pressure applied. Apparently in numberless cases there was a herd, and it did stampede. Yet in extenuation of the showing of the village, it may be urged that a considerable element stood out from the herd and exhibited a will of its own. How large a proportion it was cannot be estimated, in view of the paucity of information. But we know that the Bolsheviks experienced a bitter disappointment in respect to the Ural industrial region, where the working class stood firmly behind its vanguard, was strong in numbers and militant in spirit, and yet failed to swing the village behind it, going down in overwhelming defeat before the SR's by a margin of 664,883 to 267,577.[1] "The Urals," commissar Uritski told his party's Petrograd committee, "have not justified our expectations." [2] This is by all odds the most resounding failure to coerce or cajole peasants of which we have record.

But even in those cases where they succumbed to pressure, it

[1] Interview with the SR deputy, Tarabukin, in *Delo Naroda*, no. 242 (December 28, 1917). The Bolsheviks had counted on ten deputies but got only four (election figures for Perm province from Sviatitski's table). Remoteness from the front may well have been a factor; soldiers, for the most part peasants themselves, excelled workers as vote-getters.

[2] Trotski, *Sochineniia*, III, Part II, 364, quoted in Vishniak, *Vserossiiskoe Uchreditelnoe Sobranie*, p. 90.

must be borne in mind that the only question was whether they
would be brought over to the Bolsheviks or held in line by the
SR's. Never do we hear of their being won over, say, by the
Kadets. Indeed, in those rare instances where the Kadets had influence with the peasants it required only a modicum of agitation
to destroy that party's prestige and swing them over to the
Bolsheviks or SR's.[3] The conservative press sorrowfully acknowl-
edged that "the village gives but few votes to the party of Popular
Freedom," [4] although a prominent economist had warned its
readers months before the election that their complacency was
due for a rude awakening if they continued to regard peasant
support of the PSR as the momentary infatuation of a class
innately conservative in point of view. The peasantry in truth
had little understanding of the SR program, he wrote, and it did
have its own views, but those views in some ways were even
more radical than the party's, for the mass was quite plainly
getting ready to expropriate not only the squires (*pomeshchiki*)
but also the well-to-do peasants themselves.[5] The village was un-
questionably in a revolutionary frame of mind as it prepared to
vote, wholly unwilling to listen to conservative arguments and
uncertain only about the brand of radicalism it would take. Between radicalism and conservatism it never wavered.

Thus the malleability of the peasant will had definite limits. It

---

[3] *Derevenskaia Bednota*, no. 38 (November 25, 1917). The incident cited
occurred in Glubokovski canton, Opochetsk *uezd*, Pskov province.

[4] *Russkoe Slovo*, no. 259 (November 26, 1917).

[5] Tugan-Baranovski, "Derevnia i Uchreditelnoe Sobranie," *ibid.*, no. 163
(July 19, 1917). Durnovo in 1914 had prophesied the triumph of extremism
in the event of war and revolution; because of the nature of the Russian
people, things would never stop with a political revolution. "A particularly
fertile field for social upheavals is, of course, offered by Russia, where the
mass of the people undoubtedly embraces the principles of an unconscious
socialism . . . a political revolution in Russia is impossible, and every
revolutionary movement will inevitably degenerate into a socialistic one . . .
The Russian common man, peasant and worker alike, does not seek political
rights, which are not necessary to him, and not understandable" ("Zapiska,"
Krasnaia Nov, no. 6/10 [November–December 1922], pp. 195–196). One
can only marvel at Durnovo's depth of comprehension as well as at the
accuracy of his predictions.

could be beaten out on the anvil, but not on any anvil. And it is very easy to explain why the Bolshevik smith could often hammer it to better avail than his SR rival. A large and growing element within the PSR was becoming less and less distinguishable from Bolshevism; right after the election it would split off from the parent body and become the Party of the Left SR's.[6] Then there was the influence of Lenin's barefaced appropriation, without changing so much as a word, of the SR land program, and its promulgation as one of the first decrees of his new regime.[7] The effect can be judged from the words of an SR delegate who was explaining to a peasants' congress the surprise victory of the Bolsheviks in Moscow province: "Drunk with the destruction of Moscow, the Bolshevik garrison scattered over the countryside with Lenin's decrees in its hands and slander on its lips." [8] The Bolsheviks were promising the moon to the peasants at this time, outbidding the SR's in every particular, so that it was only natural that the simple people, ignorant of the essence of the Marxist program, should have fallen an easy prey to demagogues who carefully concealed what lay in store for them during the period

[6] The election, therefore, does not measure the strength of this element. The lists of party candidates were drawn up long before the schism occurred; they were top-heavy with older party workers whose radicalism had abated by 1917. The people voted indiscriminately for the SR label (the whole electoral process was attuned to voting by party lists instead of by individual candidates), giving only a handful of votes to SR splinter lists, whether of the left or right, in the few districts where such were offered. But inasmuch as the left-wing element controlled the party organization in some districts, it rigged the lists accordingly and mustered about forty deputies in the Constituent Assembly after the schism in late November. That is not a fair measure of its strength, however, for the leftward current was doubtlessly stronger everywhere on November 12 than when the lists had been drawn up. This whole question of the correlation of party factionalism with candidates' lists is a very complex one and cannot be treated in a study of this scope. The writer's judgments are based on his unpublished dissertation, "The Party of the Socialist-Revolutionaries and the Russian Revolution of 1917" (Harvard University, 1939).

[7] *Sobranie uzakonenii i rasporiazhenii rabochego i krestianskogo pravitelstva* (2nd ed.; Moscow, n.d.), section I, no. 1 (December 1, 1917), article 3, pp. 3–5; Lenin, "Vybory v Uchreditelnoe Sobranie i diktatura proletariata," *Sochineniia* (2nd ed.), XXIV, 640–641, and 828, n. 200.

[8] *Delo Naroda*, no. 231 (December 13, 1917).

of militant communism and the era of the Five Year Plans. Bolshevism could never have triumphed in Russia had it not been able to play upon the peasants' confused but revolutionary consciousness.

Besides the political immaturity of so large a portion of the voting public, the election may be indicted on the ground that it came off during a paroxysm of revolution and hence captured a mood that was inflamed and evanescent. In truth, each of the major parties received a substantial vote which might have gone away from it in normal times and certainly could not have been relied upon in any future test of strength. Thus the avalanche of votes for the PSR was not so much an expression of party allegiance as of the demand for expropriation without compensation; *after* the peasants had the land in their possession, they might have developed a taste for property and hence might have gravitated in the direction of some more conservative grouping. The most remarkable paradox of the election was the preponderance of rural votes in the Bolshevik column, and this was due, almost certainly, not to the consciousness of the village pauperdom — which the Bolsheviks would have claimed as their own — but to the influence of the front, either directly in the form of soldiers' votes or indirectly in the form of those of their wives and neighbors at home. The fierce agitation of peasants in uniform among those who had stayed at home flooded the urns with Bolshevik ballots. Yet this factor of war weariness, potent as it was, could only have been a transitory phenomenon: the army was in full state of distintegration and after the process had run its course and peace had been established, the village and the ex-soldiers themselves would have turned their thoughts to other matters. As for the Kadets, their middle-class and intellectual constituency had been reinforced by a rightist element which under other conditions would no doubt have gone its own way.[9] Even the Menshevik

[9] "Za neimeniem luchshego podavaite golos za spisok partii narodnoi svobody No. 1" ("For want of something better, give your vote to List No. 1, the Party of Popular Freedom"), ran the exhortation in *Fonar*, no. 10 (November 20, 1917), a newspaper published in Moscow under a

vote was not solid in that nearly half of it came from Georgia, where nationalism had long masqueraded in Menshevik trappings and where it was now about ready to doff the disguise.

But each party had granite as well as chalk in its make-up. Many peasants would have remembered the PSR as the party that gave them the land, and a tradition of support would have been built up such as is necessary to the political life of a republic; perhaps the party would have adjusted its program to the changing psychology of many of its supporters and would have retained not merely a part but nearly all of its following. The Bolshevik party had already conquered the Russian proletariat by November of 1917, acquiring a solid core around which to amass a miscellaneous following from other social groups. And the Kadets, as the standard-bearers of capitalism and Western liberalism, likewise rested on a firm though circumscribed base. Thus a free election held a few years later no doubt would have revealed a very considerable redistribution of strength without, however, reducing any of the major parties to a negligible quantity.

These two indictments of the election to the All-Russian Constituent Assembly — on grounds of abnormal timing and a prevailingly low level of political consciousness — are both serious; neither is damning. And the indictment on grounds of distortion through fraud and violence must be disallowed. The vote in question, therefore, stands on middle ground between normal elections in Western countries and the manipulated elections which have become so prominent a feature of our own day — in open form in totalitarian countries and, in other Western countries, in the restriction of the voters' choice to candidates with a similar point of view, as in the presidential election of 1940, for instance.

The significance of the election in history is, of course, bound up with the Constituent Assembly to which it gave birth. As a

---

masthead which proclaimed it to be a "patriotic paper but not at all counter-revolutionary." It was, however, beyond dispute a rightist organ, for its tone was monarchistic and it favored a limited suffrage, under which only the elite could vote. See the editorial in this issue by P. K[ochmanski]; also his article, "Za kogo sleduet podat golos na vyborakh."

political phenomenon the assembly may be considered from two opposing points of view. Either it was a victim of circumstances, a noble experiment incorporating a sound principle but doomed by the crisis into which it was born, or else it was an attempt to transplant an alien concept of government to soil where it could never flourish. Certainly the Eurasian climate has not been propitious to the growth of self-governing institutions; not free communities, but vast empires, responsive to a single will and organized on the basis of military service above and slave labor below, have been the order of the day. And this regardless of the epoch of history, the human material involved, or the ideological window-dressing provided. All we can say is that the weight of the past did not determine the results of this election; on the one occasion when they have been free to make a choice, the Russian people voted in favor of self-government. Perhaps they would not have done so the next time; perhaps the grave was ready for the experiment before it was conceived — we do not know.

The political significance of the Constituent Assembly, therefore, cannot be determined, at least not at present. But its position in history is secure. History records the failures as well as the successes of mankind — rather more the failures, one is tempted to say, than the successes — and the All-Russian Constituent Assembly, together with the election which produced it, will always be an arresting episode in the destiny of a great people, whether it marks the course to which that people will some day return, or whether it remains a lonely monument to a principle that could never germinate on the plain of Eastern Europe.

APPENDIX

To PRESENT the results of an election held in a vast, multinational empire amid the chaotic conditions that prevailed in 1917 is an intricate task. The table that follows is complex enough but many details have been suppressed. Naturally, in the work of simplification some information has had to be sacrificed. The returns have been compiled from a wide variety of sources. They are as complete and accurate as careful and long-continued research can make them. Nevertheless, numerous imperfections remain. Complete and official returns are the exception rather than the rule. For many districts the figures are known to be incomplete; for many others there is no indication in the sources as to the degree of completeness. In some cases only round figures are given; in others, the vote for certain parties is omitted. Sometimes a major portion of the vote may be announced as a lump sum without being differentiated by parties, even though one or more of the parties thus cavalierly disposed of may enjoy great local strength. And, finally, for certain districts there are no returns whatever. No claim can be made, therefore, that this is a definitive compilation. Yet it has value as the fullest and most accurate set of returns in existence.

ELECTION RETURNS BY DISTRICTS

Region and District	PSR [a]	SD Bolshevik	SD Menshevik	Minor Socialist Parties	Constitutional Democrat	Other Non-socialist Parties	Ukrainian Parties	Mohammedan Parties	Other Nationality Parties	Un-classified	Total Vote
Northern											
1. Archangel ‡ [b]	85,272	21,779	7,335	....	12,086	....	....	....	....	1,160	127,632
2. Olonets * [b]	127,062	....	126,827	....	....	....	....	....	....	....	127,062
3. Vologda ‡	320,528	67,650	....	8,071	22,912	....	....	....	....	3,742	422,903
Northwestern—Lake											
4. Petrograd Prov.	119,761	229,698	5,700	9,900	64,859	4,491	....	....	....	28,209	462,618
5. Pskov	269,267	139,690	1,952	2,440	19,026	1,828	....	....	....	6,914	441,117
6. Novgorod*	220,665	203,058	9,336	12,297	31,480	8,982	....	....	....	....	486,418
Baltic											
7. Esthonia	3,200	119,863	....	....	....	....	....	....	176,781	....	299,844
8. Livonia †	....	97,781	7,046	....	....	....	....	....	31,253	....	136,080
Western—White Russian											
9. Vitebsk *	150,279	287,101	12,471	3,599	8,132	16,602	....	....	82,354	....	560,538•
10. Minsk *	181,673	579,087	16,277	....	10,724	13,505	....	....	115,980[d]	....	917,246
11. Smolensk *	250,134	361,062	7,901	2,210	29,274	5,300	....	....	1,708	645	658,234•
12. Mogilev (no returns)	....	....	....	....	....	....	....	....	....	....	....
Central											
13. Tver †	186,030	362,687	22,552	2,338	32,830	....	....	....	....	....	606,437
14. Iaroslavl	216,744	131,124	18,240	5,014	59,400	....	....	....	....	9,412	439,934
15. Kostroma	248,951	223,353	19,529	....	41,242	17,915	....	....	....	....	550,990
16. Vladimir *	197,311	337,941	13,074	8,390	38,035	9,209	....	....	....	....	603,960
17. Moscow Prov.‡	153,458	337,492	26,877	12,586	42,415	24,546	....	....	....	....	597,374
18. Tula ‡	216,625	219,297	9,605	1,802	21,478	....	....	....	....	9,138	477,585
19. Riazañ ‡	397,229	251,815	4,389	5,216	27,808	8,773	....	....	....	....	695,230•
20. Nizhni Novgorod *	314,003	133,950	7,634	2,666	34,726	64,658	....	....	....	22,260	579,897
21. Kaluga (no returns)	....	....	....	....	....	....	....	....	....	....	....
Central Black-Earth											
22. Orël ‡	305,013	144,492	8,824	....	13,477	....	....	....	....	8,330	480,136
23. Kursk *	868,743	119,127	6,037	8,594	47,199	8,656	....	....	....	....	1,058,356
24. Voronezh *	875,300	151,517	8,658	6,116	36,488	8,027	11,871[e]	....	....	....	1,097,977
25. Tambov *	835,556	240,652	22,425	7,408	47,548	(12,460)[e]	....	6,222	....	920	1,173,191
26. Penza *	517,226	54,731	4,726	4,336	25,407	....	....	29,821	....	....	636,247

Province	1	2	3	4	5	6	7	8	9	10	Total
Southeastern–Volga											
27. Samara *	690,341	195,132	5,181	5,313	44,507	23,263	5,240	126,816	112,017[f]	....	1,207,810
28. Simbirsk	345,200	70,335	3,681	45,000	16,718	....	....	57,000	9,094	51,970	537,934
29. Saratov ‡	564,250	225,000	(11,308)	(4,606)	(20,120)	(15,211)	53,000[g]	....	....	....	954,559
30. Astrakhan †	100,482	36,023	(2,220)	....	13,017	16,400[h]	....	25,023	....	942	194,107
Black Sea–North Caucasus											
31. Don *	478,901	205,497	(6,327)	(2,620)	43,345	640,000[h]	....	....	....	29,930	1,406,620
32. Taurida †	300,150	(15,642)	(11,118)	....	(29,904)	....	61,559	60,858	....	45,519	524,750
33. Stavropol *	291,395	17,430	....	....	10,898	....	....	....	....	8,193	327,916
34. Kuban (no election)											
35. Terek-Daghestan (no election)											
36. Caspian (no returns)											
Kama–Ural											
37. Kazañ *	260,000	50,000	4,906	12,993	32,000	14,000	....	253,151	226,496	5,050	858,596
38. Viatka ‡	300,503	78,278	11,757	26,253	22,404	8,016	....	37,781	....	....	484,992
39. Perm	664,883	267,577	27,439	28,964	111,252	47,600	....	....	....	127,963	1,275,678
40. Ufa	322,276	48,135	2,334	11,442	15,653	....	....	305,121	....	259,274	964,235
41. Orenburg *	110,172	163,425	....	....	24,757	....	....	....	....	378,511[1]	676,865
Siberia											
42. Tobolsk *	388,328	....	12,061	54,513	13,793	....	....	25,830	....	....	494,525
43. Altai	621,377	45,286	3,785	6,068	12,108	17,292	....	....	8,048	....	713,964
44. Tomsk	541,153	51,456	5,769	18,488	18,618	....	....	....	....	....	635,484
45. Ienisei †	229,671	96,138	4,581	11,674	12,263	2,452	....	....	....	30,098	356,779[e]
46. Irkutsk	113,378	31,587	5,534	(6,925)	8,834	(2,653)	....	....	(15,464)	....	214,473
47. Transbaikal †	104,220	17,260	4,500	....	7,200	....	....	....	....	37,622	170,802[e]
48. Amur †	96,658	32,255	12,000	....	14,649	....	....	....	....	24,600	180,162
49. Iakutsk (no returns)											
50. Kamchatka (no returns)											
51. Chinese East. R.R. (no returns)											
Ukraine											
52. Podolia †	10,170	27,540	4,028	852	7,951	284	656,116	....	123,319[j]	....	830,260
53. Volhynia	27,575	35,612	16,947	....	22,397	....	569,044	....	55,967[k]	76,666	804,208
54. Kiev	19,201	59,413	11,532	10,089	28,630	48,641	1,256,271	....	(153,276)[l]	50,763	1,627,727
55. Chernigov	105,565	271,174	10,813	4,391	28,864	30,658	484,456	....	31,116	....	973,646
56. Poltava *	108,437[m]	64,460	5,993	48,983	18,105	61,115	760,022	....	34,631	2,102	1,149,256
57. Kharkov	650,386[m]	110,846	17,775	16,889	59,509	28,013	(see PSR)	....	13,014	....	928,526
58. Ekaterinoslav *	231,717	213,163	26,909	....	27,551	34,665	556,012	....	86,173[n]	....	1,193,049
59. Kherson ‡	354,312[m]	77,122	14,936	....	54,493	....	72,504	....	(43,608)	77,416	694,391
60. Bessarabia (no returns)											
Transcaucasia											
61. Transcaucasia *	105,265	86,935	569,362	....	24,551	....	....	....	(350,000)[o]	751,340	1,887,453

ELECTION RETURNS BY DISTRICTS (continued)

Region and District	PSR [a]	SD Bolshevik	SD Menshevik	Minor Socialist Parties	Constitutional Democrat	Other Non-socialist Parties	Ukrainian Parties	Mohammedan Parties	Other Nationality Parties	Un-classified	Total Vote
Metropolitan											
62. Petrograd *	152,230	424,027	29,167	30,728	246,506	55,456	4,219p	….	….	….	942,333
63. Moscow *	62,260	366,148	21,597	37,813	263,859	8,664	….	….	4,422	….	764,763
Army											
64. Northern Front *	249,832	471,828	10,420	5,863	13,687	….	88,956	….	….	8,669	840,591
65. Western Front *	180,582	653,430	8,000	(2,429)	16,750	(3,055)	85,062	(15,133)	(3,510)	8,669	976,000
66. SW Front *	402,930	300,112	79,630	….	13,724	….	163,354	….	….	42,673	1,007,423
67. Roumanian Front *	679,471	167,000	33,858	….	21,438	….	180,576	….	….	46,257	1,128,600
68. Caucasus Front (no returns) *	….	….	….	….	….	….	….	….	….	….	….
Fleet											
69. Black Sea *	22,251	10,771	1,943	….	….	….	12,895	….	….	4,769	52,629
70. Baltic b	15,947	43,053	….	9,736	….	28	….	….	….	….	68,764
Central Asia											
71–80. Ten districts (no election) q	….	….	….	….	….	….	….	….	….	….	….
Totals q	15,848,004	9,844,637	1,364,826	505,590	1,986,601	1,262,418	4,957,067	942,736	1,678,231	2,151,368	41,686,876r

Figures in parentheses taken from earlier, less complete tabulation.

* Known to be complete.

† Known to be only slightly incomplete.

‡ Known to be substantially incomplete (one *uezd* or more missing).

a Official lists only. Dissident SR lists included under "minor socialist." Different voting system: balloting for individual candidates instead of for lists. Vote taken is for highest candidate of each party. On Olonets, see note g to table on page 17.

b Corrected total; slight deviation from announced total. On Transbaikal, see Chapter II, note 7.

d Jewish Nationalist, 65,046; Jewish socialist, 11,064; Polish Nationalist, 36,882; White Russian, 2,988.

e Joint list: Ukrainian SR, Left SR, and Polish Socialist Party (PPS).

f German Nationalist, 47,705; German Socialist, 42,156; Bashkir Federalist, 13,100; Chuvash, 9,056.

g Joint list, Ukrainian and Tatar.

h Cossack vote. On Don Region, see Chapter II, note 8.

i See Chapter II, note 12.

j Jewish Nationalist, 62,547; other Jewish, 13,860; Polish, 46,912.

k Two Jewish lists.

l Jewish Nationalist, 86,943; Jewish socialist, 35,443; Polish, 30,890.

m Joint list, Ukrainian SR and SR.

n Jewish Nationalist, 37,032; Jewish socialist, 14,021; German, 25,977; Greek, 9,143.

o Armenian Dashnaktsutiun. See Chapter II, note 18.

p Joint list, Ukrainian socialist bloc and Jewish Socialist Workers' Party.

q Exclusive of joint lists herein indicated.

r Total by districts and also corrected total by parties (represents addition of 126,827 from Menshevik column to foregoing totals by parties, but with deduction of 126,827 from Menshevik column to eliminate overlapping with SR vote in Olonets district).

BIBLIOGRAPHICAL NOTE

THE literature on the Constituent Assembly is not extensive and for the most part concerns the history of that body rather than the election which produced it. The three studies made of the election itself — those of Sviatitski, Lenin, and the Archives of the October Revolution — have been mentioned in the text (see pp. 4–5).

It had been the official intent to publish information pertaining to the election in the bulletins of the All-Russian Electoral Commission (*Izvestiia Vserossiiskoi po delam o vyborakh v Uchreditelnoe Sobranie Komissii*). But since this organ was a creation of the Provisional Government, it came into conflict with the Soviet authority after the October Revolution, its work was seriously hampered, and eventually it was suppressed. Preparations for the election as well as the opening phase of the controversy are described in the bulletins, and beginning with No. 24 (December 16, 1917), returns were published by districts. Unfortunately for the student of history, however, this most important of statistical sources is abruptly terminated with the next issue (December 20, 1917), leaving a valuable but fragmentary record of the reports from district commissions. The last two numbers containing returns are exceedingly rare and it is doubtful that even Sviatitski saw them.

The cessation of official reports and the incompleteness of the statistical data presented by Sviatitski and the Soviet Archives throw the investigator back upon the only two remaining sources of information: the press and local accounts of the revolution. Although provincial studies began to be published early in the Soviet period, most of them appeared about 1927–28 in connection with the tenth anniversary of the October Revolution. Uneven in quality and not infrequently marked by a low level of performance, these accounts nevertheless reward the student who has the time and patience to go through them; the better ones shed a good deal of light on the election campaign in the province under consideration and may even present a tabulation of returns. It is to be regretted that for some provinces the events of 1917 have never been written up.

As for the press, the search for election data is not unlike looking for a needle in a haystack. The more obvious reports are likely to have been worked over by Sviatitski, though not necessarily so — nothing can be taken for granted when one is dealing with the election to the All-Russian Constituent Assembly. The Soviet press is not as helpful as it could have been, considering the vantage ground which it occupied: as opinion in government circles became increasingly hostile to the Constituent Assembly, less and less space was devoted to the election in the columns of Bolshevik newspapers and a campaign of depreciation set in. This is particularly true of *Pravda*; as for the *Izvestiia Tsentralnago Ispolnitelnago Komiteta i petrogradskago soveta*, its coverage of the election is uniformly disappointing, in the beginning as at the end.

The opposition press, especially the nonsocialist press, labored under the disability of being hounded by the new regime just at the time that returns were coming in. Thus the newspaper which published more detailed information than any other, the *Russkoe Slovo* of Moscow, was suppressed outright at the end of November. The *Russkiia Vedomosti* of the same city managed to keep going during the whole period of voting; its observations on the election are the most trustworthy of all, but statistically it leaves something to be desired. The best treatment of the election in a socialist newspaper, with respect both to figures and comment, is to be found in the Petrograd *Delo Naroda*, the central organ of the PSR. Other metropolitan newspapers yield less information than those mentioned, but there is always the chance that some item was included in one paper which did not appear in the others.

There is no doubt that a study of the election would be enriched by a systematic survey of the provincial press, but the materials are so dispersed and inaccessible that they virtually defy inspection. Even where it has been possible to consult the files of a local newspaper, the value of the investigation has been lessened by missing numbers. Enough was found, however, to indicate the fruitfulness of this source if the obstacles to its exploitation could be overcome.

There is also no doubt that the central archives could be made to yield more than they have thus far at the hands of Soviet scholars. But in view of the ravages of war and revolution and the lapse of time, it seems unlikely that the complete record of the election can be assembled, even under more favorable circumstances than hitherto have prevailed.

INDEX

Administrative system, units of, 3*n.*

All-Russian Commission on Affairs Pertaining to the Election of the Constituent Assembly, 3, 49–50

Archives of the October Revolution, report of proceedings of Constituent Assembly, 4–5; apportionment of seats in Assembly, 20–21; lack of data on village vote, 64

Arkhangelsk, electoral returns, 12

Armenians, in election of 1917, 20

Army. *See* Soldiers

Bakhmut, death of Menshevik mayor, 47

Balloting, difficulties of, 2–3

Ballots. *See* Party lists

Baltic, constituted naval electoral district, 35

Baltic Fleet, electoral returns, 12; propagandists of Bolshevik cause, 40–41

Baltic provinces, analysis of electoral returns, 33–34

Bashkirs, in election of 1917, 19–20

Bessarabia, electoral returns not found, 6

Black Sea Fleet, constituted electoral district, 36

Black-earth region, analysis of electoral returns, 26–27

Bolsheviks, supplant Provisional Government, 3; tenets of, 7; in election of 1917, 14; in Novgorod province, 24; in Vladimir, 25; in Kursk, 26; in Kazañ, 28; in Tomsk, 29; in Ukraine, 31; in White Russia, 32–33; in Esthonia, 33; in Petrograd and Moscow, 35; in army and navy, 36–37; strongholds of, in election, 38; supported by Baltic Fleet and military, 40–42, 55–56, 61–62; electoral hostility to, 42–44; loss of election, 46–50, 52; effect of revolution on, 54–55; workers' support of, 56; in Kozlov *uezd*, 58–60, 63; peasant resistance to, 61, 63; in Saratov province, 69; influence on peasantry, 71–73

Bourgeoisie, in Petrograd and Moscow, 35

Canton, defined, 3*n.*

Caucasian Front, figures deleted, 13; Bolsheviks and Socialist Revolutionaries, 37

Central Asia, elections not held, 6

Central industrial region, analysis of electoral returns, 24–26

Cheremis, in election of 1917, 20

Chernigov, electoral returns, 12, 13; Bolshevik party in, 55–56

Chinese Eastern Railroad, electoral returns not found, 6

Church. *See* Clergy

Chuvash, in election of 1917, 20; in Kazañ province, 27

Civil servants, hostility of, to Bolsheviks, 35

Civil war, correlation with election, 40

Class, as factor in election, 23

Clergy, eclipse of, in election, 18; in Kazañ, 28; hostility to Bolsheviks, 42–43

Communication, disruption of, 3

Constituent Assembly, difficulty of reconstruction, 1–2; abortive nature of, 2; report of proceedings, 4–5; vacancies, 6; apportionment of seats, 20–21; town and country attitudes, 62; as political phenomenon, 74–75

Constitutional Democrats, tenets of, 9–10, 51; in election of 1917, 15, 18; in Novgorod province, 24; in Vladimir, 25; in Kursk, 27; in